LOTTA JANSDOTTER

EVERYDAY STYLE

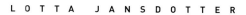

LOTTA JANSDOTTER

EVERYDAY STYLE

KEY PIECES TO SEW
+
ACCESSORIES, STYLING & INSPIRATION

PHOTOGRAPHY BY JENNY HALLENGREN   STC CRAFT / A MELANIE FALICK BOOK / NEW YORK

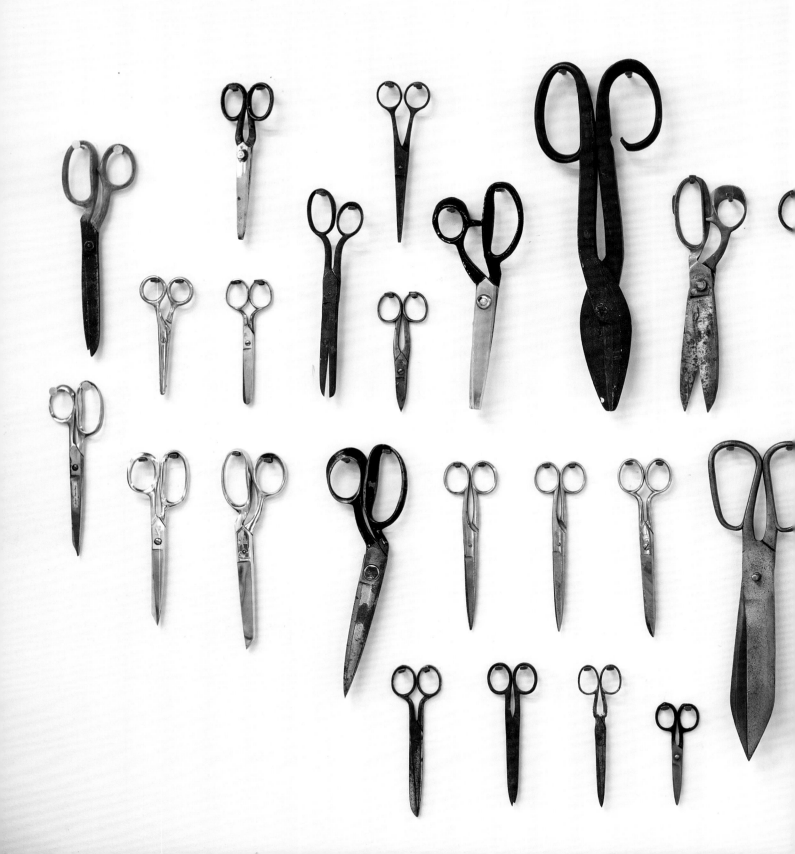

CONTENTS

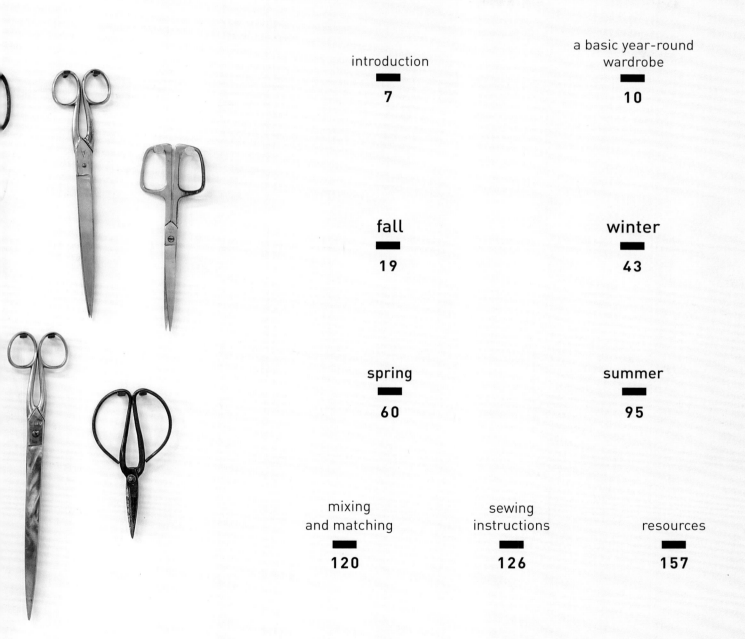

Introduction

More than eight years ago, I penned *Simple Sewing*, my first sewing book. My goal was to encourage people to sew simple but inspiring projects by providing them with easy-to-understand instructions. I wanted to show people how gratifying sewing can be, even if it's just making a tea towel by hemming a piece of fabric with a straight stitch. I wanted readers to feel the wonderful sense of satisfaction that I feel when I make something by hand, all by myself—something I can give away or use and wear in my everyday life.

A lot has changed for me since *Simple Sewing* was published. I have written more books, moved from San Francisco to Brooklyn, had a baby boy, moved my studio five times (argh! New York City real estate!), traveled near and far, and collaborated with many companies in many different ways. I have designed a gazillion different things and collections. I have done a great deal of work and experienced marvelous rewards, some hard lessons, and yes, many changes.

Yet some things are still very much the same for me. Here I am, writing another sewing book, and still I maintain the very same values and approach: I aim to inspire people to make simple, useful objects to be treasured.

During the past decade I have connected with so many of you. I've met you at workshops and openings. You've shared tips and suggestions, hugs and handwritten letters, and photos of your sewing projects. Many of you have commented on how I dress and asked me about my "style," wondering where I buy my clothing or if I sew it myself. It is all most flattering. Thank you. I have written *Lotta Jansdotter Everyday Style* to answer those questions about what I wear and how I have developed my style.

Well, yes, I love clothing, and I know what really works for me and what I like. The pieces that I wear have clean lines and are usually very functional, easy to move in, cute (but not too cute), a tad tomboy at times, and mostly rather timeless.

I enjoy shopping at different designer shops here in Brooklyn and discovering new shops when I travel. I invest in a few special pieces and then combine them with thrift-shop finds as well as basics from mainstream clothing stores.

But how about making garments for myself?

How nice it would be to actually make my own clothing, to select sewing patterns and fabrics and trims and make garments that are a true reflection of me and my style! Doing this was rather common—a norm rather than a novelty—a half-century ago. My grandmother Sylvia made garments for all five of her children, sometimes even out of old linen sugar bags. My grandmother Anna and my aunt Kina did the same. Kina designed her own garments and sold them out of her amazing shop for years. When I was seven years old, she made a bridesmaid's dress for me, and when I wore it I felt like the prettiest little girl ever created.

There was also that other special dress made just for me: my wedding dress. The very talented Karin Mosseri in San Francisco designed the most wonderful dress, interpreting my ideas and half-finished sketches so beautifully. The cut, the shape, the fabric: All of it was such a perfect reflection of me and my personality, and I felt remarkable wearing it. And yes, for the second time, I did feel like the prettiest girl in the world. I loved my wedding dress so much that I asked Karin to make me another one after the wedding, exactly the same but in gunmetal gray.

I love handmade clothing, but to this day I still have only beginner sewing skills. I don't know why I didn't learn to sew from my grandmothers and aunt. I only picked up the basics in home-economics classes when I was nine years old back in Sweden.

But why limit myself in this way? I decided that I could write this book by collaborating with someone with the skills I lack and, along the way, I hoped that I would learn to sew better. Fortunately, I found the very talented Alexia Abegg.

I set a schedule to write and photograph this book in a little over a year. I began with my sketchbook, where I wrote down the ideas and inspirations that came to me at home, at work, and while traveling. I took home pages from magazines. I copied links online. I thought about the clothing I already owned that I loved to wear most and the accessories that made them the most versatile. I fabric-shopped and took home swatches. I doodled. All this thinking and recording made it possible to define what I thought would make the best basic year-round wardrobe. My goal was to design pieces I would wear myself but that would also appeal to all kinds of people—short and tall, young and old, living and working in all kinds of places.

Alexia marvelously interpreted my ideas, making them better by sharing her technical skills and creativity, producing patterns for an everyday wardrobe that I love—one that is functional, versatile, and easy to sew and alter. And that is exactly how I like it!

Now please join me, so we can sew together! Don't be shy if you are a beginner. It is never too late to begin, and the patterns in this book are a great place to start. I cannot wait to see what you make, especially how you translate these patterns and make them your own. Experiment with different fabrics, play around with the details, and, hopefully, be inspired. I look forward to receiving your photos and notes and to meeting in person.

A Basic Year-Round Wardrobe

There are so many different styles and trends, each one lovelier than the next. I set out to design a wardrobe and then I was a bit overwhelmed for a few moments there. In the end, it was very easy though, once I reminded myself to keep it simple, of course!

There are five core garment patterns in this book, each one easy to understand and adaptable. The jacket becomes the coat, the shorts become the pants, etc. So, with these five patterns, you can really create twelve different silhouettes. Once you start changing fabrics, adding pockets and other details, and layering, the sky is the limit.

**TEDRA SKIRT
INSTRUCTIONS
PAGE 128**

SKIRT

1. short

2. medium to knee

3. long. ankle

J A C K E T + C O A T

1. jacket

2. coat

PILVI JACKET/COAT
INSTRUCTIONS
PAGE 00

S H O R T S   +   P A N T

1.

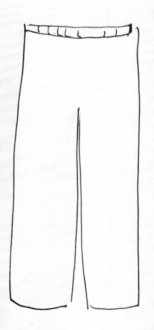

2.

TOP + DRESS

1.

2.

KIOMI TOP/DRESS
INSTRUCTIONS
PAGE 131

Paula in top
86–87

Nerissa in dress
88–89

Maddy in dress
90–91

Lotta in dress
98–99

Lotta in top
102–103

TOP + TUNIC + KAFTAN

1.   2.   3

B A G S

wilma

Cecilia

Astrid

Elsa

I had to include several bag patterns in this book because, of course, the bag is the most important and useful fashion accessory of all.

Choosing Fabrics

I have countless piles of fabrics in my studio and at home in fun patterns and gorgeous colors: irresistible sari silks from the market in Ahmedabad, old woven linens from a market in Riga, thick cotton from my favorite department store in Stockholm, and naturally, bolts of the many fabrics I have designed. While I am not a fabric expert, I know what I like and what I think works well for my projects, including the sewing patterns in this book. Here are some basic guidelines to get you started.

General Guidelines

If you are new to garment sewing, use reasonably priced fabric that does not slip or stretch, such as cotton, linen, or cotton-linen blend (my favorites, by the way). To test the garments for this book, Alexia first made all of them in muslin, a cost-effective plain-weave cotton. Once we were sure we liked the style and the fit, she made them again in our "hero" fabric.

If you have never sewn a garment before, avoid silk, rayon, and shiny polyester, because they slip and slide. Avoid cotton jersey and other knitted fabrics, too, because the garments in this book were designed for wovens.

In general, I find that thin fabrics work best for tops and dresses, and heavier fabrics are more suited to pants, skirts, and jackets.

Cotton

Cotton is versatile, comfortable, comes in many different weights, and is usually reasonably priced. The term "quilting cotton" generally refers to a medium-weight cotton made for quilting and is also commonly used for home décor items and accessories, such as pillows and bags. It can be used for garments as well, but because it is stiffer than apparel cottons, it works best for structured garments that need a little body. It comes in about a zillion prints. Sewing with this fabric is incredibly easy: It's easy to cut, doesn't slip and slide, holds a crease, and irons nicely.

Linen (flax)

Linen is a cool and absorbent fabric that is easy to sew. It comes in a variety of weights as well as blended with cotton and other fibers; it is often used for summer clothing and home décor. It wrinkles easily and can be a tad expensive.

Silk

Silk has a smooth, soft texture that can be slippery; less-expensive synthetic fibers meant to simulate silk even more so. It is comfortable and absorbent but wrinkles easily. Silk is one of the strongest natural fibers but loses up to 20 percent of its strength when wet. Sometimes it needs to be dry-cleaned. Prices vary.

Wool

In the fabric world, the term *wool* is used for fabric made from the fiber of different animals, including sheep, goats, rabbits, and alpacas. Wool is strong, warm, and dry, and it doesn't wrinkle easily. While some wool can be coarse and itchy, high-quality wool is usually soft. It comes in many different weights and is best dry-cleaned.

Rayon

Rayon is made from purified cellulose, primarily wood pulp. Rayon is a versatile fiber and is widely claimed to have the same comfort properties as natural fibers. It can imitate the feel and texture of silk, wool, cotton, and linen. Many people recommend dry-cleaning rayon, but you can indeed wash it by hand.

fall

Back in 1996 I started my company, "Lotta Jansdotter," out of a tiny storage space in the basement of the building where I was residing in San Francisco. I screen-printed and sewed pillows, table linens, and totes that I sold in shops in town. I had discovered screen-printing at a community college and knew almost immediately that I had found my medium.

As a child growing up in Sweden, and as a young adult finding my way in the States, I always loved to draw plants and flowers and other patterns, and now I had found a way to print them... on fabric. Fast-forward many years, and I am still creating patterns for a living. Today they are printed on fabric by the yard as well as on table linens, bedding, paper goods, wrapping papers, bags, and porcelain, among many other things. And, yes, I also like to sew and write books.

I now live and work in Brooklyn, New York, a fascinating place full of creative people and great food. Life moves fast here and at times it feels a bit overwhelming. But mostly, it is a fun town with great things to do and see.

My studio is filled with books, art materials, stacks of fabrics, magazine clippings, and far too many piles of papers. This is where I spend most of my weekdays, collaborating with many different companies to create products with my designs printed on them.

I create all my patterns by hand, cutting papers, drawing with pen or India ink, and block printing. A direct connection with real materials is an important part of my process. I want to touch the paper and hear it crinkle, feel my scissors slicing through it. I like getting my fingers sticky with rubber cement, and I don't mind getting ink under my fingernails. I try, with great effort, to stay away from the computer as much as possible when I create—I make all my designs by hand.

Fall is always an especially busy time in my studio. This is the season when I plan new fabric collections and often create new designs. After a long summer break, I am always bursting with ideas.

Here I am wearing the Esme Tunic with tights in the fall. This tunic is made out of the softest hand-woven raspberry colored fabric.

Using a contrasting fabric for the pockets would also look great!

I bought the fabric through my friend Maja who once interned in my studio and now works for Camphill Soltane, a nonprofit that supports and teaches skills to young adults with developmental challenges. The fabric was made at Camphill Soltane, and I love knowing that it was woven by someone who put great care and effort into the process.

The raspberry color is just perfect for me as it's not too bright or too muted.

This is the kind of casual, no-fuss look I like to wear when I'm working in the studio. I can lift, bend, sit, and skip in this thing.

I opted to topstitch pockets on this tunic, which are rather handy for measuring tape, lip balm, rubber bands, and other bits and bobs I like to have close by. I also like wearing this tunic with a pair of jeans or black pants.

fall

Truth to be told, I probably have all the bags that I need: back-packs, purses, sacks, hobos & messengers.

Nevertheless, I wanted a super-simple tote to use every day, one big enough for my laptop and my lunchbox but not too big or bulky. I wanted a tote I could take to the studio that would also be appropriate for a business meeting and could transition into a spontaneous evening out.

The Elsa Everyday Tote Alexia and I designed has nice rounded corners, so it feels a bit more finished and sweet and, well, not so square. The leather handles and the grommets we used help the bag hold up to heavy content. I chose a very simple, but rather gorgeous, thick linen for this bag. The fabric is a special weave that I scored in a remnant shop. I think canvas, or even waxed canvas, would work great for this tote as well.

The bag is dark navy blue because it is a color I really fancy right now, and it truly works with almost every other color and pattern in my closet.

namaste
my name is Jerry

SHOBHANA FABRICS®
Exclusive Dress Material & Ethenic Wear
Shop No. 191/192, 2nd Lane, Mangaldas Market, Mumbai - 400 002.
E-mail: shobhanafabrics@gmail.com

No Exchange • Claimless Goods

Cash Memo No. 19033   Date: 4-10-13

M/s.

100 Print Fab 3.00×1   300
300 Hot Fab 3.00×1   900
                             1200

SHRI NAR
Wholesaler &
6, Khanda,
Chou

M/s.
550
240
40

Note :- 1. O
2. N
3. T

Dot designs

Lucky
Lucky

for necklaces ?

October in India

I had longed to visit India, and last fall I finally got the chance to go there to teach color and design workshops to local artisans and to tourists. Every day for two weeks my senses were bombarded by patterns, scents, buildings, trash, vehicles, people, cloth, and cows as well as all the challenges and rewards of living life in India. It was a wonderful and magical sensory journey.

It was, of course, also fun to explore all the different traditional garments in India. The women's saris are truly amazing, and there is an astounding array of patterns, colors, and qualities to choose from. A sari can cost anywhere from $20 for a very basic one to $3,000 for an extravagant one. Tunics are more practical for daily wear, combined with pants, and are worn by both Indian men and women. I bought far too many tunics and cotton kurtis (long, loose cotton shirts) and salwar pants, which are loose pajama-like pants. I wear these tops and bottoms together and also mix and match them with my jeans, sweaters, jackets, and long skirts.

I also loved the many kinds of necklaces, flower garlands, and beads I saw everywhere. Plain cotton string, paper, beads, bells, tassels, and plastic petals—they were all tied or strung together in one way or another, often to be used as decorations at celebrations and ceremonies.

In Jaipur we got a private tour of a traditional dye house where they dye silk and cotton using a sort of tie-dye process. I was fascinated by the way the fabric was tied before it was placed in the dye bath. And yes, we rode on elephants, happy elephants that were well taken care of. Mine was named Lucky and that is also the name of the fabric collection I designed based on this trip.

Inspired fashion INDIA

a lot of layers

texture and color

Block printing on slow days; calm, sunny on the porch in Jaipur India

october 2013

poms

fall

27

fall

Back home in Brooklyn, I unpacked stacks of fabric, strand after strand of wooden beads, hand-carved combs, and more fabric. I was eager to use my new materials to make necklaces and bracelets. But I needed some help, so I reached out to my dear friend Annika Inez, a very talented jewelry designer who has her own jewelry company in Brooklyn called ByBoe. To make the bracelets shown here, we used a wide array of fabrics in different widths and some bracelet hardware. To make the tied ones on pages 32 and 33, we used strands of cut silk onto which we added metal beads. These pieces are so simple to make and look great individually and together.

ribbon crimp
hardware

interfacing

lobster
clasp

Making Fabric Bracelets

You will need: fabric, interfacing, fabric glue, ribbon crimp hardware, jumprings, clasp, & needle-nose pliers

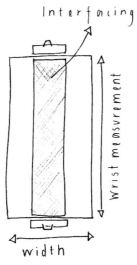

Interfacing

Wrist measurement

width

1. Measure your ribbon crimp hardware.

2. Cut the fabric to twice the width of the crimp hardware.

3. Measure your wrist & cut the fabric to that length.

4. Cut the interfacing to the width of the crimp hardware by the length of your fabric.

5. Iron the interfacing to the center of the wrong side of the fabric.

A

B

6. Apply a thin coat of fabric glue to the interfacing.

7. Fold fabric edge A over onto the glue.

8. Apply another thin coat of fabric glue to edge A, then fold over edge B. Press firmly and let dry.

9. Use needle-nose pliers to flatten the crimp hardware over the ends of your bracelet. Add jump rings & a clasp.

Here Annika is wearing the Pilvi Jacket in soft, black wool for nippy fall days.

This black wool fabric has itsy-bitsy white polka dots that add texture. The style of this cropped jacket is a bit "Jackie O"—classic, midcentury, proper. Annika is more of an urban, bohemian, rock 'n' roll kind of lady, but I love how she made it work for her with a simple gray T-shirt and jeans.

In this variation, the top front corners of the jacket are stitched down to create the look of a small collar. Another option is to add snap buttons instead of permanent stitching on each side; that way you can wear the "collar" up or down.

I asked my friend Lauren to model the Pilvi Coat. Lauren and I know each other through our kids, who go to the same school. They used to be BFFs. These days the kids are, sadly, not really hanging out together that much, but Lauren and I took a liking to each other and we "stuck." Now we go on long walks by the water or enjoy a drink together every now and then.

Here the Pilvi Coat is made in thick, gorgeous, and I must admit, expensive white wool. White looks classic & distinctive, but it is an unexpected choice these days. It reminds me of movie stars & first ladies from the forties & fifties.

And yes, isn't it funny how very much Lauren and I look alike? I mean, I always ask her where she cuts her hair, and where she buys her boots. And when I asked her to model this coat in her way, she was wearing her black jeans and black top . . . just I like I do with my coat on page 68. So funny—I love it. I think her casual outfits are the perfect fit with this classic coat: It is a nice, and needed, contrast that takes down the "serious properness" it might exude otherwise.

Making Fabric Necklaces

I wanted the necklaces below and on pages 40–41 to be a mixture of fabric, string, beads, pompoms, and other found bling and treasures. For some reason, my usual belief in simplicity does not really apply when it comes to jewelry. With these necklaces I wanted to be playful, mix it up like crazy, and be eclectic. Of course, wearing just one necklace at a time is fun, too

You will need: fabric, interfacing, string or ribbon, fabric glue

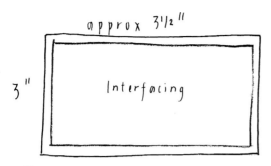

approx 3½"

3"

Interfacing

① Cut a piece of fabric as shown.

② Cut a piece of interfacing slightly smaller than the fabric, and iron it to the center back of the fabric.

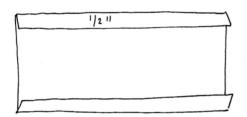

½"

③ Fold & press the long edges of the fabric. Use fabric glue to glue down the edges.

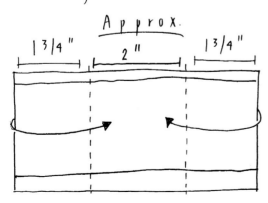

Approx.

1¾"   2"   1¾"

④ Fold in one short end as shown. Press & repeat with the other short end, overlapping the first.

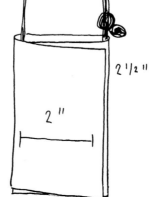

2½"

2"

⑤ Tuck in the ends of a string or ribbon for the necklace. I like adding a bell or bead to the string. Glue down the fabric flaps, securing the string ends in place.

½" (1.3 cm)
1¾" (4.4 cm)
2" (5 cm)
2½" (6.4 cm)
3" (7.6 cm)
3½" (9 cm)

my handmade porcelain leaf pendants strung on cord.

Sewn fabric strand with one big eye-catching bead.

Mini
pom poms
sewn
onto
cord.

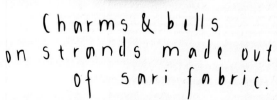

Charms & bells
on strands made out
of sari fabric.

winter

Ahh, Stockholm in the winter. It can be rather cold and dark. The days are short, and the winter months are very long. That long darkness can be challenging to live in. But when there is snow on the ground, it lights up the town, and when the sun does, indeed, decide to peek out, those winter days can be truly inspiring.

The stillness and beauty of the winter landscape can also be very grounding. My grandmother always said, "There is no such thing as bad weather; there are only bad clothes." So, as long as I am dressed warmly, I don't mind spending a lot of time taking walks outside in the nippy cold. The bare trees reveal themselves and offer me a chance to take a close look at their structure and texture. I can see the different shapes formed by the bare branches. I love the pale, somber blue and gray colors and the pretty patterns formed by the ice and snow. During these walks my mind roams and my imagination is refreshed.

In my design work I tend to create spare and organic shapes, and when I look back at my collections over the years, I so easily see the influence of that stark Scandinavian winter landscape. Even though right now I spend most of my winters in New York, my creativity seems forever connected to my roots and those walks.

winter

When I went back to Stockholm in February while working on this book, I visited with Maria, one of my oldest and dearest friends, and her family. Maria is an illustrator, teacher, and a real great mum to three fabulous kids.

Maria & I often take long walks together that last for hours, be it rain or shine, summer or winter.

This is something we started doing as teenagers, and over the years we have shared many ideas and thoughts on our strolls.

One of our favorite walks takes us to a communal garden called Winterviken, located a tad outside the Stockholm city center, right by the water. There is a lovely restaurant there, and we make sure to stop for our sacred Swedish *fika* time.

Maria is wearing a short version of the Tedra Skirt. The fabric is a salt-and-pepper speckled wool with a great nubby texture. Together with a classic striped Marseille shirt, this is a cute outfit, and I like the belt as an added accent.

This skirt easily teams up with chunky sweaters and big boots for winter or with a blouse and some oxford shoes for when warmer spring weather comes along. The topstitched pockets on the skirt are a nice and rather practical addition.

winter

47

↑ wrap yarn around the disks.

↓ template made out of card-board.

I brought lots of yarn with me when I visited Maria and her family. My idea was to make really big, oversized pompom hats, inspired by the Sami people in northern Sweden. The Sami (Lapps or Laplanders) are the only indigenous people of Scandinavia. The Sami have a rich, deep history and strong traditions in handicrafts. They make beautiful clothing that is often adorned with ribbon work or embroidery, unique leather boots, and various kinds of hats. It was one of those hats that got my attention. The hat was fun and playful, and I simply loved the kooky, oversized pompom that adorned it.

winter

trim
your
pom-
poms.

many
colors
&
different sizes.

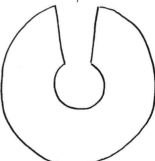

Making Pompoms

You will need: cardboard & yarn

① Make two cardboard disks using the template shown here. Stack the disks (like a bagel sandwich).

② Wrap yarn around the disks. The more yarn, the thicker the pompom.

③ Wiggle your scissors in between the two disks, and cut the yarn around the outside edge.

④ Cut a piece of yarn & place it between the two disks; use it to tie the wrapped yarn pieces together tightly.

Pompom Template

Trace this template and cut two cardboard disks. (cereal boxes work well). This template makes a pompom about 1½" (3.8 cm). For larger pompoms scale up the template to the size you like.

Making Wool Cuffs

Trace my simple template onto a piece of paper & use that as your pattern. The size of my hands is fairly normal (I would think) - they are size medium. You might need to adjust the sizing to fit your hand. Use cheap felt fabric to work out the sizing before sewing your cuffs in wool.

The cuffs I'm wearing on page 42 couldn't be easier to make. Each one is basically a tube cut out of soft, warm wool. Choose a rather thick wool so the cuffs hold their shape—a boiled or tufted wool would work as well. The pattern does include a little curved shaping so the cuffs fit naturally and stay up on your wrist.

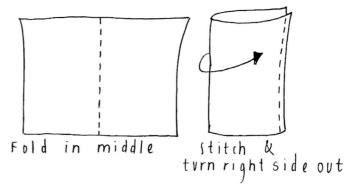

Fold in middle   stitch & turn right side out

① Fold in middle.

② stitch & turn right side out.

Please note: The cuff template is not square; the angles help shape the cuff for a better fit.

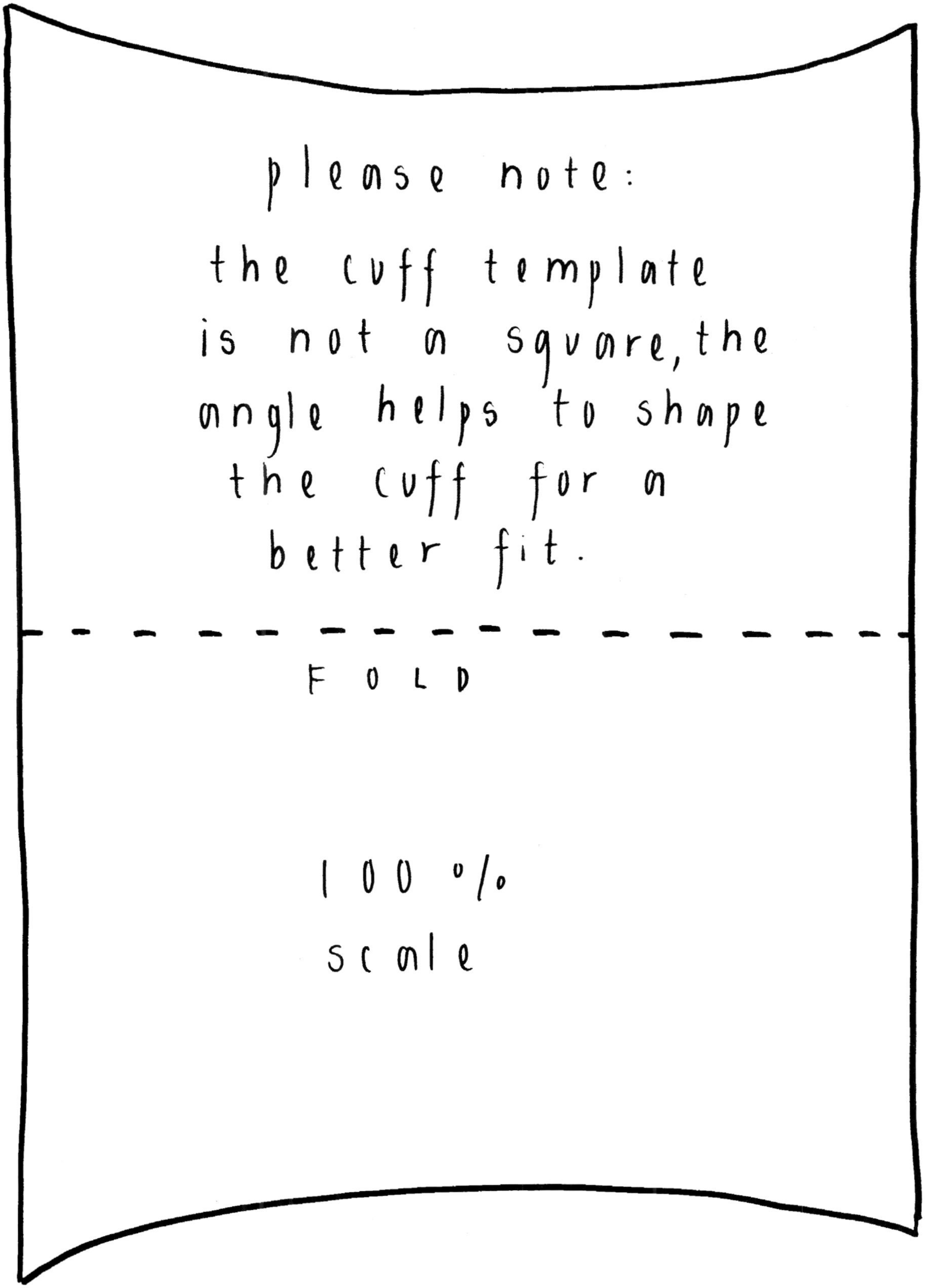

please note:
the cuff template
is not a square, the
angle helps to shape
the cuff for a
better fit.

‐ ‐ ‐ ‐ ‐ ‐ ‐ ‐ ‐ ‐ ‐ ‐ ‐ ‐ ‐ ‐

F O L D

1 0 0 %
scale

When I see Olga, I cannot help but think of a gorgeous, mythical elf straight out of the classic John Bauer fairy tales. Olga is a lovely twelve-year-old who has so much much wit & grace.

She is the daughter of a good friend of mine in Stockholm. Olga studies ballet and is very interested in photography. I love that Olga already has her own unique style. She often goes ice-skating wearing classic, Swedish hand-knitted *Lovika vantar* (mittens) and an old pair of men's skates that have been in the family seemingly forever.

Her style truly came forth when I asked her to model the Tedra long wool skirt. She paired it with a simple gray angora sweater and hand-knit hat for a classic, monochromatic look that works so well for her. Her favorite Doc Marten boots added a nice contrast.

This wool skirt is a very good basic. The gray color makes it easy to combine with various other colors, and you can go wild with patterned tops, since the solid gray will anchor the outfit. The clean cut creates a good base that you can combine with form-fitting polo shirts, flowing blouses, or layered tops.

Sunny was my intern in my Brooklyn studio last spring.

Here she is wearing the Esme Top sewn from one of my cotton fabrics and the Owyn Pants sewn in a thin, luscious, washed linen that makes them very comfortable for yoga. The pants have an elastic waist, so they work well for activities and movement.

Sunny studied graphic design and interned for me because she wanted to learn the ins and outs of running an independent design studio. It turns out that Sunny is also a certified yoga teacher, which tickles me since I dabble in, and love, yoga. I asked her to show me some of her favorite postures.

Who says yoga-wear has to be Lycra?

I find most yoga bags a bit unwieldy, and carrying a rolled-up mat on its own just doesn't work for me, especially when I bike. So I did some research and came up with a bag style that makes the mat (and some clothing) easy to carry.

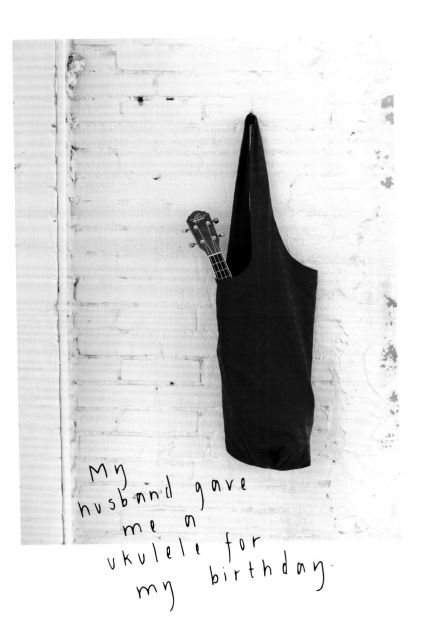

My husband gave me a ukulele for my birthday.

I recommend that you make the Cecilia Yoga Bag in a thick, sturdy fabric, such as canvas. I am quite happy with mine. Who says it needs to be used for only yoga mats?

Spring is the most welcome season, for obvious reasons. We've made it through the cold winter, which in Brooklyn often means snow days, delayed subway trains, and a rather frigid studio. I can't deny that I'm glad when winter is over. The milder temperatures draw me outside into the fresh air for walks and bike rides. I feel energized and free and newly inspired.

Last spring I visited Alexia, who collaborated with me on the sewing patterns in this book, in her hometown of Nashville, Tennessee, so that we could spread out and work together in person. Nashville is a great town in the spring. It's not too hot, not too cold. You will probably be comfortable as long as you dress in layers or bring a scarf. Alexia runs her business, Green Bee Patterns, from there with her husband, Rob, and her mum, Michelle. Alexia is a splendid and generous hostess. She took us to only the tastiest restaurants, where I ate some of the best tacos and ice cream (not together) I have ever had. We also visited fabric stores and coffee shops.

After my visit with Alexia I felt even more confident about our plans for this book. It's true that we can get a lot done with computers and the Internet but, in the end, working together side by side is always the best.

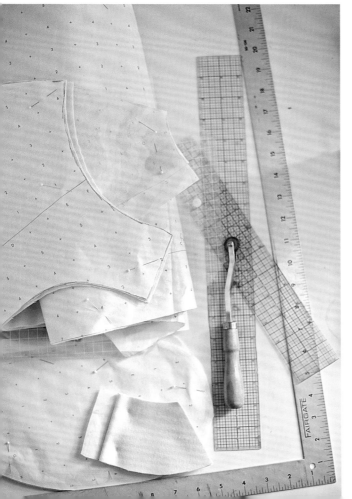

I first met Alexia and her mom at a trade show in Houston. They were selling their cute sewing patterns, exhibiting them in an even cuter booth that they had created. I was charmed by them and very impressed with their work. We started talking, and I quickly felt that Alexia could be a perfect fit for this book.

Not only did I think she would understand my style, I believed she could translate my ideas into real garments that I would want to wear every day. And I think she is one of the nicest people I have met—and I like working with nice people!

In Nashville, Alexia introduced me to her family of creatives, who all love making things with their hands, be it music, quilts, garments, photographs, collages, or sketches. Michelle taught her three daughters to sew. Alexia's father, Jimmy, invited us to his studio one afternoon, and I was completely disarmed by his sincere and contagious passion for his art and his creative process. I never wanted to leave that studio.

Alexia & Michelle are finishing up the last stitches in the hem of the kaftan, so I can take it with me on my upcoming trip to Mexico.

I wanted to start painting on the spot, even though I'd never painted before. My days are already full with a gazillion projects, and Alexia and I had sewing to attend to that day, so no painting for me. But one day soon, Mr. Abegg, I shall pick up a brush and start painting. Thank you for stoking that fire.

In Alexia's studio, we worked out the styles and final fit for the garments in this book. I picked fabrics for the garments, and Alexia showed me which pieces had to be cut on the bias and explained why. I learned a lot on that visit and had a marvelous time. Thank you, family Abegg, for all your help and for everything. I will treasure my visit for a very long time.

spring

Alexia and I are each wearing the Esme Tunic in our own way.

Alexia opted to make her tunic in a textured chambray fabric and to wear it with leggings and a scarf. Most likely, the sturdy fabric we used for my dress (which I found at a big Swedish furniture store you might be familiar with) was intended for drapes or other home décor items. I adore big, checkered fabric patterns, so this tunic has quickly become a favorite that I wear too much already. I say too much since I am worried I am going to wear it out (but wait, I can always make another one!). I am wearing the tunic as a dress paired with another favorite: the leather boots I invested in eight years ago. They made their first appearance in my book *Simple Sewing*.

Here I am wearing the Pilvi Coat made from my own cotton fabric as I head out to do some fabric shopping back home in New York. It is a perfect "coverall" over my black jeans and top, a staple outfit of mine. This coat adds some color and a bit of security when I feel those jeans might be a wee bit too tight over my assets.

One of the real pluses of living in New York City is having access to crazy - good fabric & notions stores.

New York's iconic Garment District is sadly shrinking, as smaller shops are being taken over by bigger and more commercial stores. But there are still old-fashioned gems to visit (for a list of some of my favorites, see page 157).

What's very exciting and assuring are all the independent, modern, curated fabric stores sprouting up in New York and around the country. I think I can safely say that Purl in the SoHo neighborhood of New York City was one of the first of its kind when it opened in 2002. This place is endlessly inspiring, stocked with only the best notions, fabrics, and sewing patterns.

Purl is where I venture when I need that something extra for my projects, when I am looking for a perfect detail, a certain look, a specific color of embroidery thread, or that unique fabric. The shop is rather brilliant for that. So when I created the projects for this book, I immediately steered my steps toward Purl for pompom fringe, luscious yarns, amazing Japanese gauze fabric, and cool binding tape in smashing colors and patterns.

spring

As you know, I design fabric and surface patterns. One of the main trade shows for my industry is Quilt Market, which takes place every summer and fall. Here, I launch and sell my fabric collections, along with many other textile designers. This is where retailers gather to buy fabric and everything sewing, including machines, scissors, batting, patterns, thread, and much, much more. And yes, there is *a lot* of quilting going on here.

I like to quilt, but I don't do it very often. I am one of those quilters who likes to work quickly and can't be bothered to make things straight or perfectly aligned. As a *wabi sabi* sort of person, I prefer the perfectly imperfect. So I sew my pieces together quickly and in an organized mess, though the few quilts I have made came out all right. I am a very big fan of the improvisational quilts made by women in Gee's Bend, Alabama, so that probably says something about my quilting style.

During the year I was working on this book, the spring Quilt Market took place in Pittsburgh, a city I was excited to visit for the first time. In preparation for that show, I got the idea of making a patchwork scarf as a small, wearable project. So I reached out to some talented ladies in the world of sewing and invited them to make the scarf their way for this book. You can see the scarves on pages 74 and 75. They were all made the same way but each one is unique and each one is awesome.

Yes, Webster is indeed rather over-weight, but a real happy & sweet fat cat

I invited
four savvy
& talented
friends of
mine to
make their
own version
of the
patchwork
scarf

& look
at these
beauties...

mine

Carolyn Friedlander
used different kinds of
blue fabrics for hers.

Amber's

Jamie's

Christine
Haynes
used
a lot
of soft gauze
fabric & fun trim.

The ladies that own &
run Fancy Tiger Crafts in Denver
made such creative & fun ones.

Making a Patchwork Scarf

You will need: fabric, ribbon or twill tape, bias tape, thread
I recommend using fabric that looks good on both sides.

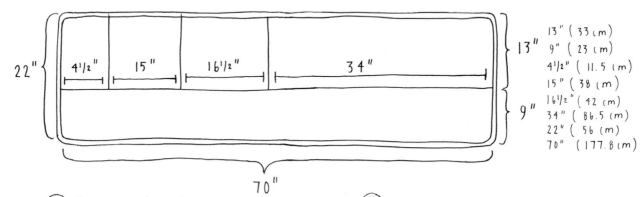

22"
4½"   15"   16½"   34"
13"
9"
70"

13" (33 cm)
9" (23 cm)
4½" (11.5 cm)
15" (38 cm)
16½" (42 cm)
34" (86.5 cm)
22" (56 cm)
70" (177.8 cm)

① Prewash all your fabrics.

② Cut out all your pieces, as shown above.

③ Start with sewing all your smaller pieces together; right sides of fabric facing each other.

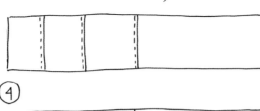

④

Sew the two large pieces together.

⑤

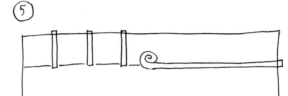

On the back side, place ribbon or twill tape over the seams and topstitch in place.

⑥ And to finish,

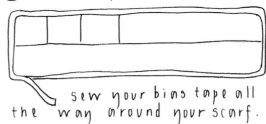

sew your bias tape all the way around your scarf.

Width of bias tape is up to you, but ½" (1.3 cm) width works nicely for this.
To get rounded corners, you can trace the circle shape onto the fabric using a round jar or can.

I am very happy to introduce you to my lovely mother-in-law, Patty. A remarkable woman in every way, she is a Renaissance person who makes & creates to no end.

Patty is a sculptor with many exhibitions in her past and in her future. She makes great cakes, she has sung in choirs all her life, she is an avid quilter, and she's not afraid to fix the plumbing or a broken screen door if needed. I've even seen her cobble her own shoes—in the car no less! Not only is she talented, she's also a riot. And yes, Patty is very, very good at sewing. Her attention to detail and absolute perfectionism are amazing. It's no wonder I seek her out to help me with my sewing projects.

Patty is wearing the Esme Tunic sewn from my Lina fabric. It is a very graphic print, and I love how easily Patty pulls it off, combining it with her favorite tights and scarf. It is bold, energetic, and playful— just like Patty.

spring

79

I'm now able to crank out scarves for many different occasions & moods in a jiffy.

I visited Patty and asked her to help me with a few of the smaller sewing projects in this book. First, I wanted to make these scarves, with inspiration lingering from my trip to India. And then I asked her to help me create the Patchwork Bias Tape on page 82. I like that both of these accessories are easy to make.

Making a Triangle Scarf

You will need: fabric, pompom trim, thread

I recommend using a woven fabric that looks good on both sides, such as linen or silk; or if you are lucky to find a fabric that is printed on both sides, that will work well, too.

① Prewash your fabric.

② Cut your triangle. The size is up to you and is determined a bit by the width of the fabric.

Fold fabric over & cut.

And then you simply sew on your pompom trim around the edges of your scarf.

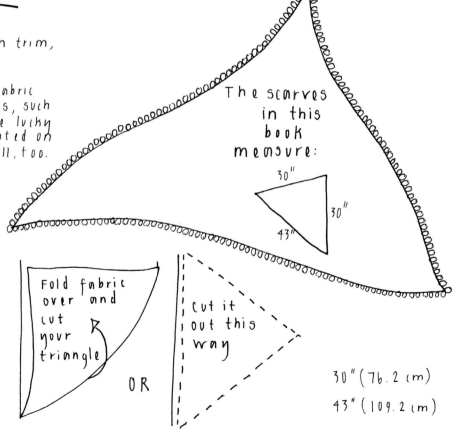

The scarves in this book measure:

30"
30"
43"

Fold fabric over and cut your triangle

OR

Cut it out this way

30" (76.2 cm)
43" (109.2 cm)

Making Patchwork Bias Tape

You need: fabric, bias tape maker, & thread

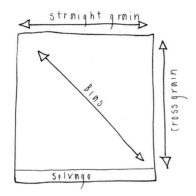

straight grain

Bias

cross grain

selvage

① Cut your fabric on the bias by cutting it at a 45-degree angle to the selvage. The fabric has the most stretch on the bias. Cut the strips to the width recommended for your bias tape maker and to all different lengths.

② When you have plenty of scraps, sew them together right sides facing into a long strip.

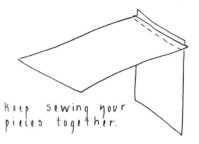

Keep sewing your pieces together.

③ When you have your desired length, press all seams open.

④ Feed your tape through your bias tape maker following the instructions that came with it.

bias
tape
makers

Use your
leftover
fabric scraps
& make
some
rather
fun & useful
bias tape

Pich

PAJARO

traditionell floral
motif.
embroidery

backside
of
tunic
add
a few
flowers
@ bott

Flam-
vongan

April in Mexico

In the photo on page 64 you can see the linen Esme Kaftan Alexia and Michelle worked on in Austin. It is plain and simple, in the best way, and reminds me of a Scandinavian farmer's shirt from the 1850s.

I brought that kaftan with me on a trip to the Yucatan in Mexico. I was invited there to facilitate color, design, and product development workshops with a group of embroidery artisans.

Right away, I was completely smitten by the ladies and their beautiful handicrafts; they can truly do magic with their hands and thread. And all the ladies were wearing traditional embroidered dresses that were stunning and vibrant. I, too, wanted to walk around in one of those embroidered beauties, so out came my plain "farmer's kaftan." But I now wanted to transform it into a pretty Mexican garment! I sketched a design in my journal and asked the ladies to help me. I stayed with one color of thread, though—I am Swedish, after all. Going with a dozen vibrant colors would be a bit bold for me. (You can see me wearing my "new" Mexican Esme Kaftan on page 97.)

Of course, Mexico was also inspiring in many other ways: the warmth of the people, the celebration of color in everyday life, the handmade tamales. I will definitely go back to explore more of their native design and handiwork, the weaving, architecture, and all the hand-painted tile.

My friend Paula is wearing the Owyn pants sewn from an indigo blue cotton fabric. Nothing fancy — it's just basic, practical fabric that holds up to many washes, since Paula wears these pants all day in the clay studio.

Paula is one of the most creative and talented people I know. She can make great things from whatever she touches, and right now she's touching a lot of clay. Paula makes wonderful vessels and platters in distinct shapes and with her signature pattern— stripes. We first met in a beginner ceramics class a few years ago. Today she's a very successful clay artist whose work sells out as soon as it hits the shelves. OK, I have a little designer crush on her, and she has all my respect and admiration.

Paula's Kiomi Top is sewn from a thin white canvas, which gives it a utilitarian feel and makes it perfect and practical for work. This is an easy and functional outfit that you can move in, made with materials that can handle wash after wash. For variation, we made this Kiomi Top with a contrasting bias tape at the neckline and armholes.

I asked my friend Nerissa to model the Kiomi Dress made in black silk.

While sewing with 100-percent silk may seem scary, this dress turned out *so* great. It drapes and flows beautifully. And it fits my dear Nerissa perfectly, as it did a lot of different friends who all ended up wanting it.

 Nerissa is a talented musician and my right hand. She has worked with me for well over eight years, and without her I am helpless in so many ways. She is my trusted confidante and a constant source of advice, clever solutions, and skills. She is also a crazy-fun dance partner when two-stepping in Houston.

 A great basic black dress is a wardrobe staple in my mind. This is a dress you can wear over a pair of jeans and still feel classy and dressy in it. It's suitable for an evening of drinks at the Plaza (I wish) or, in Nerissa's case, for a performance in Manhattan or Perth. Thanks to a suggestion by Alexia, we added small loops and made a thin belt to define the waist.

spring

I love this dress!
It is elegant & simple
and yet incredibly
comfortable & smart.

Linen fabric breathes, so a summer dress made from this fabric makes sense. It's perfect for muggy, hot summer days in Brooklyn when you almost can't stand the thought of wearing anything at all.

"shuggi"

Maddy was our boy's sitter a few years ago. She is a spunky, vibrant, and wicked-smart young lady. She began sewing when she was eight years old and started her own fashion company when she was nineteen, creating a line of custom-made women's blazers. She was granted a Thiel Fellowship to develop The CRATED, a digital content site that provides information about starting a fashion business to new and up-and-coming designers. She is off on exciting adventures in life and almost always with a big smile on her face.

Maddy is wearing the Kiomi Dress, cut to a mid-length, sewn from 100-percent linen from Lithuania. I know some people say you have to dry-clean linen to prevent it from shrinking, but I love the feel of linen after a hot wash. It gets softer each time, and it drapes a bit nicer after a few washes as well. What I do is prewash my linen fabric prior to sewing. That way, it is pre-shrunk before I sew with it.

spring

Here is a giant version of the Elsa Everyday Tote. I loved playing around with the scale on this one. Yes, it is a wee bit oversized, but it's so fun! It makes a real statement, if you are into that sort of thing, and it holds a lot.

I love rags rugs and grew up with them in Sweden.

As a kid, I remember rag rugs on the floor of every summer house, and my grandmother and uncle made their own for years. So I decided to mix my childhood memories with modern chic by making a bag from a rag rug.

The rug I used was pretty soft and not too thick, so it was easier to sew than it

looks. Just be sure to overlock or zigzag the cut edges so they don't fray. Use leather handles and grommets to ensure this big tote holds up to wear and tear.

spring

summer

My summers are spent back home in Scandinavia with my dearest friends in Sweden and my family on the Åland Islands, located smack in the middle of the Baltic Sea. I pack too many things, and my boy and I go away on our summer sabbatical to unwind, play, and immerse ourselves in nature. We spend lots of time by the ocean, in the ocean, and running around barefoot. It's freeing to unplug and simply relax.

I absolutely need to reconnect with my heritage and family in this way in order to recharge and then be able to constantly move forward with new ideas—and be brave—when I'm back in New York. Next summer we will build a very small, very special summer house there, a place where even more ideas and inspiration will be born.

Growing up in Scandinavia, I spent a lot of time, especially durning the summer, in nature, surrounded by sparse fields, vast ocean landscapes, and the muted colors of rocks, weath-ered barns, and hay. I picked flowers and drew flowers. I made things with sticks and leaves. I harvested carrots and potatoes with my uncle and loved getting my hands dirty.

I have fantastic childhood memories that I treasure; these mem-ories bring me security and comfort. They remind me how important it is to disconnect from technology, to step away from the e-mails that never stop coming, to stop making too many plans, and to embrace that space of "nothingness" and just be.

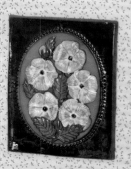

This kind of easy summer living calls for easy summer wear. I don't need a lot of fuss—just a basic dress that I can pull over my head.

The big, long Kiomi Dress serves this purpose and that of personal changing booth: I can swiftly change into my swimsuit while wearing this dress. It's brilliant!

My Kiomi Dress is sewn from my 100-percent cotton quilting-weight fabric, which has just enough body to add some structure without being too stiff. This sunny stripe simply screams summer and is so fun to wear.

Evenings in Scandinavia get cool, and mosquitos can be fierce, so you might need to top your dress with a cardigan. I sometimes wear leggings for added warmth, but they're easily hidden by the generous Kiomi Dress.

I think this dress would look awesome paired with some chunky boots and a sweater in fall. But, as you can see, it's lovely with bare feet, too.

summer

våra fina svalor
var i afrika bor
de på vintern?

svarta vinbär Norrgårds 2014

vattenfärg
blomma

August on Åland

I have been keeping visual journals and sketchbooks for almost as long as I can remember. As a little girl I must have drawn thousands of flowers, fields, animals, and princesses with pretty, patterned dresses. I also enjoyed having many pen pals from around the world, and when I sent out their letters, I always decorated the envelopes with borders and ornaments. I wonder what the mail carriers on different continents thought of all of my doodles.

My drawing habits have not changed significantly since back then. Today I use the most basic tools. I favor two simple black pens (never pencil), one thin and one bold. I like that strong, permanent mark, and I often let the pen lead me and my hand across the paper. One of my favorite techniques is creating cross-hatched patterns and textures. It feels good to do and looks nice. I also like filling in spaces with soft watercolors.

During my summers in Sweden I often sit by the ocean, just taking in all the beauty and calm, listening to the chirping swallows. The sun does try to set during those gorgeous light-filled evenings, creating gorgeous golden colors across the sky. All this finds its way into my sketchbook—and my designs—one way or another.

I like to cook when I have time to do so. And during summer vacation I have ample time.

I'm wearing the Kiomi Top, this time sewn from another of my 100-percent cotton fabrics. Here you can see how it flares a bit at the bottom. The pants are ones I wore all summer: the Owyn Pants made from shiny viscose cotton sateen fabric. The pants are black, which means I can pair them with anything: T-shirts, tunics, clogs, tank tops, sneakers, sweaters, and high heels in fun colors. OK, I admit, I rarely wear high heels, but I think you understand what I am getting at. The shininess of this fabric took me by surprise, and I am really surprised by how much I ended up loving it. I am a matte, natural kind of gal, but this shiny black was a welcome change. It just proves that one should try different things sometimes, even when it comes to fabrics.

summer

Gun Skytt lives in the same village as Jenny & her family.

Gun is a sweet, delightful, and energetic eighty-six-year-old who invited us over for coffee and princess cake. Princess cake is a cream-filled cake covered with green marzipan, topped with a pink marzipan rose. There's no pastry more Swedish than princess cake; it's a true classic and ridiculously tasty. Gun shared stories with us about the fun she had during the 1940s dancing with the many handsome soldiers whose boats docked in the harbor. Gun really loves to dance.

Gun is wearing the Pilvi

Jacket sewn using one of my soft canvas fabrics. The canvas makes the jacket feel sturdy and more structured. And I think this turquoise green really suits Gun. She wore it over her favorite blouse, and I love how the ruffles of the blouse complement the simple neckline of the jacket. It's a nice detail that says a lot about Gun's personality. This cropped jacket works so well combined with a knee-length skirt, as Gun shows us here.

summer

Fanny is also a resident of Jenny's village and the daughter of a good friend. Fanny is a high school student, an avid hockey player, and a natural beauty—clearly. There is no concealer or makeup in sight. We met Fanny at the village boat harbor where she and her family reside in a remodeled boathouse during the summer months. Fanny is close to getting her driver's license, but until then, Grandma's old bike will help her get around.

Fanny is wearing the Esme Top. For this version, I used a thin cotton fabric I stumbled upon on the closeout shelf in a department store in Puerto Rico a few years ago. This fabric is perfect for a casual top. I am incurably drawn to yellow and white fabric and to fat plaids, whether they are on trend or not! I think yellow and white pairs well with so many other colors, and it's flattering on most people as well, no matter their coloring.

The Owyn Shorts are sewn from a soft denim chambray. Denim chambray is much lighter in weight than denim used for jeans, so it's more comfortable and not as bulky. It is also a great deal easier to sew. We added some belt loops for these shorts, which are practical, of course, but also lend a nice visual detail. The belt loops would be cute in a contrasting color, or you could make all the belt loops the same color except for one. Fun!

My friend Anna Linda was born to wear kaftans.

When I thought about creating a kaftan, my thoughts went to the 1970s. People wore a lot of kaftans back then, and they looked great. I knew I definitely wanted a kaftan for myself, and I wanted one for Anna Linda too.

Anna Linda is a child of nature who's in tune with most everything. She is a trained researcher in science and business management, has a black belt in aikido, and is a speaker and business consultant.

She looks absolutely stunning in the Esme Kaftan made from equally stunning Nani Iro fabric. Anna Linda is a tall, slender woman, and a kaftan works well for ladies with that build. She can carry the length of the kaftan well, like a Greek goddess but in a Swedish hippie sort of way.

The shape and construction of the kaftan is so simple that it is almost like a blank canvas. It is the perfect garment for big patterns and motifs, and since it's usually worn on beaches and on holidays, you can go wild with vivid colors as well.

I fell in love with this Nani Iro gauze fabric as soon as I saw it. Nani Iro is a Japanese designer whom I have admired for years. Her designs are produced in Japan, often on this light double-gauze fabric that is soft and cozy, sheer and airy, but not see-through.

A few years ago
I was flipping through
a magazine when I
spotted this big ol'
tote bag that looked
so cool & handy.

It had what seemed to be a simple construction and nice wide handles, and it was made from a lovely linen burlap that made me think of country living in Provence. That bag stuck with me for years. Then, while making this book, I explained the bag to Alexia, who fabulously interpreted it into the Wilma Tote. I love it. I chose a heavyweight linen fabric that reminds me of France; we fused the lining to it for extra support.

Here I am carrying my laundry in the Wilma Tote, one of the many excellent ways to use it. And look, I'm wearing my favorite shiny pants again—on laundry day no less!

In Stockholm
in August, the
evenings are
already much
darker & the
air has a
different
scent.

The first inklings of fall are
creeping in. Some days you
can still get away with summer
garments, but then suddenly the
weather calls for knitted sweaters
again.

We visited our friend
Caroline one Wednesday
afternoon for (you guessed it)
coffee. Caroline lives in an old
building from 1924 in the central
part of Stockholm. She runs her
own company that sells organic
children's clothing, and the
precious pieces are made from
the best materials in wonderful
colors.

Caroline has a great appetite for books, and I discovered so many titles that I can't wait to start reading. Caroline also has an amazing collection of natural- and nude-colored shoes in all shapes and styles.

Here you see her nude oxfords, a pair of shoes I wish I also owned. I love how she paired these simple shoes and a natural sweater with these brightly patterned Owyn Pants. It's a good meeting of two very different looks.

I found this fabric in Puerto Rico, and I was so attracted to it that I bought more than six yards. It reminded me of tiles in Morocco. And that vibrant blue is so handsome. At first I thought it would be great for a tablecloth, but look how well it works for pants! I love it. And I have so much of the fabric that I can make a tablecloth, too.

The Owyn Pants are awesome to wear during the day, but they could easily become your favorite pair of pajamas, too.

The idea to add a little something to the Owyn Pants Paula wore on page 86 came when I found this woven ribbon at a yard sale.

I love how the black-and-white graphic feels modern and traditionally Scandinavian at the same time. Sewing on the ribbon took me a while, but it was worth the extra effort because the pants feel so different now—not better, necessarily, but different. I like it.

There are so many ways to add fun elements to your garments. How about adding a swatch of fabric to a skirt hem? It has absolutely no function whatsoever; it's simply fun. Or instead of adding an element, try taking one away. Rather than hem your skirt, leave the edge raw and let it fray. The Tedra Skirt made in chunky dark denim would be ideal for this look.

Adding a decorative element can change up a garment.

Yunmee is truly
an original lady

The Esme Tunic I brought for Yunmee to wear was one Alexia made in a rayon fabric as a test. I spotted the tunic in Alexia's house in Nashville and pleaded to borrow it for the shoot. Little did we know that this Australian kangaroo and the tunic would look so good together! I love these photos; they are dreamy, wacky, and sweet—just like Yunmee.

Rayon is a fairly new fabric to me. I am very curious about it, and I suspect I will start using it more. It is breathable and comfortable to wear with a nice loose drape. It does not build up static cling nor will it pill. But it can stretch easily when wet, so be careful when you wash it. Dry-cleaning really is the best way to go.

She's an illustrator & artist in Brooklyn who went to art school in London with my best friend Maria.

I made her acquaintance again when Maria invited her to a group exhibition I hosted in my studio one spring. Yunmee brought many unique and lovely prints to exhibit along with an Australian tree kangaroo she created from papier mâché and felt. He spent the whole weekend perched on a big wooden ladder in my studio, and by the time we packed up the show, I was completely smitten with that guy. So I asked Yunmee if she and her Aussie friend would model in my book. We spent one rainy morning at the local café eating pie and taking pictures.

I love hands-free and I love small & compact.

We all need one good small bag for those quick errands around the corner or for an evening out when we don't need more than our wallet, keys, and phone. The Astrid Cross-Body Bag fits the bill and also allows us to carry our belongings hands-free, which is ideal when reading a book, riding a bike, or holding coffee.

This bag is made from my Ruta quilting-weight cotton fabric, so it needed a lining. But you can use a thicker fabric and skip the lining altogether if you prefer.

I like combining leather with fabric, and grommets are the way to make the two work together. I love how the bag looks with my Esme Tunic and Owyn Pants.

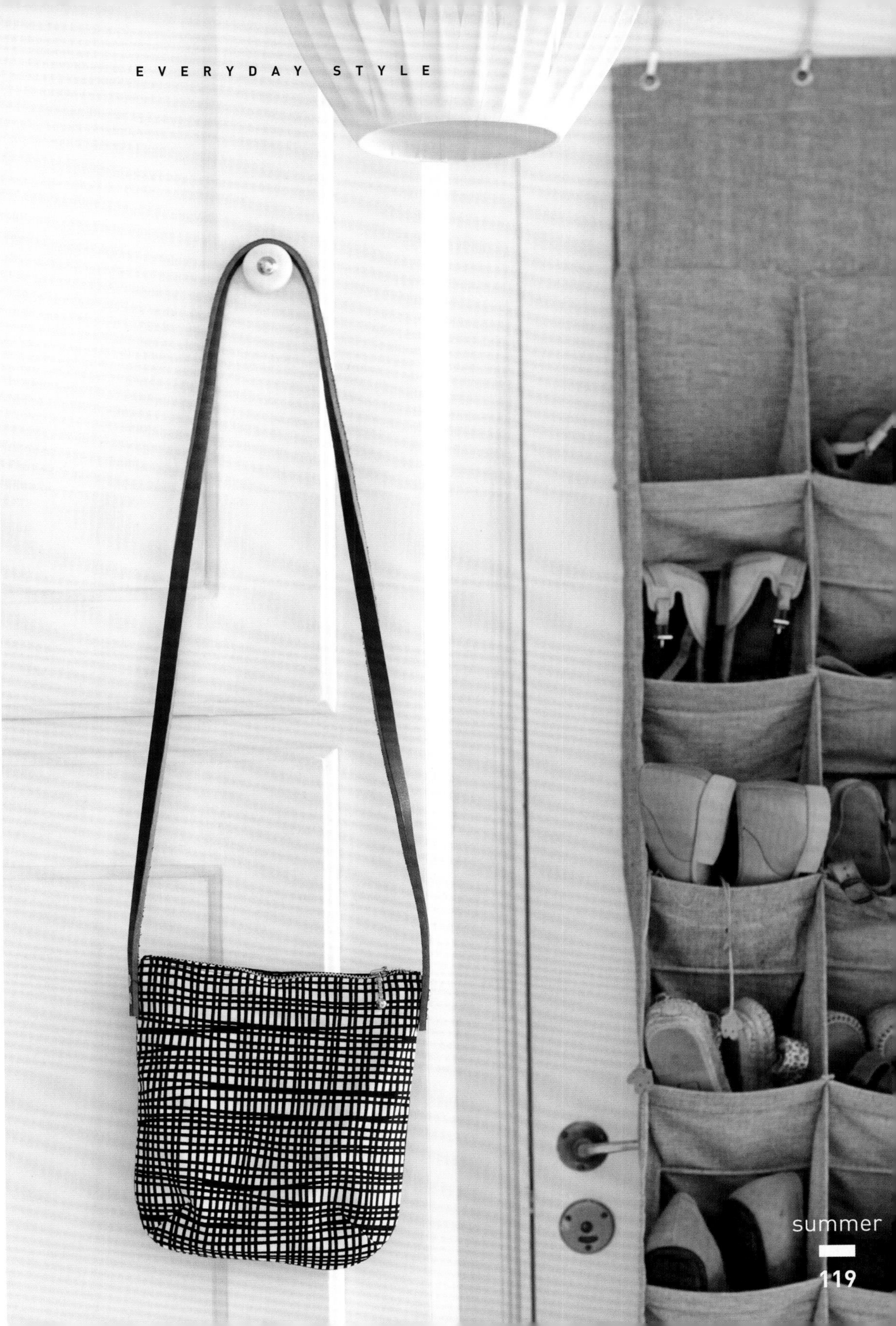

Mixing & Matching

On fall days I can
still use my favorite
Esme Tunic.
I combine it
with jeans &
a cardigan.

The Esme Top
+ jeans=
an easy &
casual
combo

I love this bold & simple color combo! My dark blue Kiomi Top with the white Pilvi Coat & orange Owyn Pants.

Inspired by India, I layered my silk Kiomi Dress with my shiny Owyn Pants.

A basic turtle-neck combined with the Tedra Skirt is a great "everyday at work" outfit for me.

The Owyn Pants again! This time together with the Pilvi Jacket & a Kiomi Top.

Even the linen Esme Kaftan will work in the fall.

I just pulled my favorite sweater over it.

And yes, that's my grand-mum's old fur hat.

I love layering!

I am wearing the Esme Top together with the wool Tedra Skirt — another easy combo.

Sewing Instructions

The projects in this book are functional, versatile, and easy to sew and alter, and are a great place to start if you've never sewn garments or bags before. Before you begin, allow me to share some general information.

How to Use This Book

Pattern Sheet Guides

To use the patterns included in this book, first refer to the instructions for the garment you'd like to make, identify the pattern pieces required for the project you are making, and then use the Pattern Sheet Guides on pages 152-155 for help locating which sheet your pieces are on. Once you find those pieces on the pattern sheets, trace them using tracing paper, pattern paper, or tissue. Transfer all markings such as notches and darts. Some of the pattern pieces are divided onto more than one pattern sheet, so use the lettered and numbered matching guides, along with the outer border lines on each pattern sheet to correctly align the sheets when tracing.

Fabric Cutting Guides

Within each project instruction, we have provided fabric cutting guides. These guides show the best way to place your traced patterns on the fabric for cutting. The black in these illustrations indicates the fabric right side, the gray indicates the fabric wrong side, and the white indicates the pattern pieces. Note that the fold line and fabric selvages are also marked. Place the pattern pieces on the fabric exactly as shown; occasionally you will need to flip the pattern piece over to place it as indicated on the guide.

Sewing Basics

Preparing Fabric

When you purchase your fabric for a project, you may consider purchasing a bit more to allow for shrinkage after the fabric has been washed. Check the information given by the fabric manufacturer for the percentage of shrinkage to be expected and multiply that number by the total yardage required to determine how much more fabric to purchase. When you get the fabric home, wash and dry it just as you would the finished garment (if you plan to dry-clean the garment, then dry-clean the yardage).

Cutting Fabric

Place your traced patterns on the fabric as shown in the fabric cutting guides that accompany each project. Use pattern weights or pins to hold the patterns in place. As you cut, be sure to keep all the fabric on your cutting surface; the weight of fabric hanging off the side of your table could distort your cut fabric pieces.

Marking Tools

As you cut the fabric, transfer all the markings from the pattern to the fabric. For this job, I like to use a fabric marker, tailor's chalk, or chalk transfer paper and a tracing wheel. The markings that are important to transfer are darts, notches or dots used for matching corresponding pieces, and fold lines for casings.

Seam Finishing

After you have cut your garment pieces from the fabric, you may choose to finish the raw edges before you start assembling the garment. Finishing the edges will ensure a professional-looking finish and will make your garment more durable. To finish the raw edges, use a zigzag or overcast stitch on your sewing machine, or an overcast stitch on your serger, to simply sew all around the cut fabric pieces. Once the edges are finished, follow the instructions that follow to make the garment.

Seam Allowances

As you assemble the projects, note that the seam allowance for each is ½" (12 mm), unless otherwise indicated. This means that you'll sew your seams ½" (12 mm) from the edge of the fabric. The patterns and measurements given here include the seam allowance, so there's no need to add them.

Interfacing

Some of the garments and many of the bags call for interfacing, which we attach to the fabric to add body. We recommend Shape-Flex by Pellon because it's thin enough to move with the fabric, but it's durable and isn't too stiff or crisp. Shape-Flex is a fusible interfacing, which allows you to simply iron it to the wrong side of your fabric wherever it's needed. Follow the manufacturer's instructions for the proper heat setting for your iron.

Facings

Many of the garment patterns include facings. These sections of fabric finish edges on necklines, armholes, or waists and then remain on the inside of the garment. Facings allow the garment to fit and drape properly when you wear it.

Clipping

When working with an area of a sewing project that has an inside curve when finished, like a neckline, you will need to clip into the seam allowances from the edge of the fabric to very close to the stitched seam, being careful not to cut the stitching. These cuts allow the curve to lay flat and should be made every ½" to ¾" (12 mm to 2 cm) along the curved seam edge.

Notching

When working with an area of a sewing project that has an outside curve, such as the lower curved edges of the Astrid Cross-Body Bag (page 144), you will need to notch into the seam allowances from the edge of the fabric toward the stitched seam. Stop just before the stitching, cutting out a small *V*-shaped piece of fabric from the seam allowance. These cuts will allow the curve to be

smooth and lay flat. Make these notches every ½" to ¾" (12 mm to 2 cm) along the curved seam edge.

Topstitching

This line of stitching helps to strengthen the seam and adds a decorative touch to your project. It can also help to hold a facing in place or finish a hem. Because the topstitching will be seen on the outside of your garment or bag, you may choose to use a contrasting thread, to show off the stitches, or a matching thread, for a more subtle look. Backstitch at the beginning and end of your topstitching.

Staystitching

Staystitches are straight stitches sewn through one layer of fabric, which serve to stabilize fabric edges around necklines or where a zipper will be placed. Sew staystitches within the seam allowance; since the seam allowances in this book are ½" (12 mm), sew your staystitches ⅜" (1 cm) from the fabric edge. Backstitch at the beginning and end of your staystitching.

Size Chart

The chart below lists bust, waist, and hip measurements meant to help you determine which size garment to make. Use a standard cloth measuring tape measure to take your measurements while standing barefoot and wearing the undergarments you plan to wear under your new item. To obtain the bust measurement, wrap the tape over the fullest part of your bust and straight across your back. To obtain the waist measurement, measure at the natural dip in your waist, or the part of your waist where you want your garment to sit. And finally, to obtain the hip measurement, measure your hips at their widest point. Match your measurements to the garment size to which they pertain.

SIZE	BUST	WAIST	HIPS
XS	32"–33½" (81.3 cm–85.1 cm)	24½"–25½" (62.2 cm–64.8 cm)	35½"–36½" (90.2 cm–92.7 cm)
S	34"–35½" (86.4 cm–90.2 cm)	26"–27½" (66 cm–70 cm)	37"–38½" (94 cm–97.8 cm)
M	36"–37½" (91.4 cm–95.3 cm)	28"–29½" (71.1 cm–74.9 cm)	39"–40½" (99.1 cm–102.9 cm)
L	38"–40½" (96.5 cm–102.9 cm)	30"–32" (76.2 cm–81.3 cm)	41"–43" (104.1 cm–109.2 cm)
XL	41"–43" (104.1 cm–109.2 cm)	32½"–34" (82.6 cm–86.4 cm)	43½"–45" (110.5 cm–114.3 cm)

Tedra Skirt

Unlined bias-cut skirt in three length variations with side invisible zipper and Petersham ribbon-faced waistband. Short skirt has optional pockets.

VARIATION 1:
Short bias-cut skirt with pockets

VARIATION 2:
Medium-length bias-cut skirt with raw edge hem

VARIATION 3:
Long bias-cut skirt

½" (12 mm) seam allowance used unless otherwise indicated.

FABRIC CUTTING GUIDES

SHORT
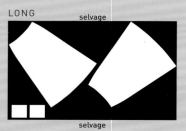

MEDIUM
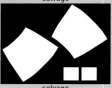

LONG
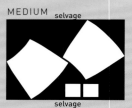

SUPPLIES

All Variations

Wool crepe, lightweight wool suiting, textured mid-weight wool, denim, mid-weight cotton, cotton double gauze fabric. Not suitable for diagonal prints.

1 yard (90 cm) 2"- (5 cm-) wide rayon Petersham ribbon

9" (23 cm) invisible zipper

All-purpose thread

Short skirt with pockets
1⅝ yards (1.5 m) fabric at least 44" (112 cm) wide

Medium-length skirt with or without pockets
1¾ yards (1.6 m) fabric at least 44" (112 cm) wide

Long skirt with or without pockets
2½ yards (2.3 m) fabric at least 54" (137 cm) wide

TOOLS

· Pins
· Scissors
· Wash-away fabric marker or chalk
· Zipper foot for sewing machine

PATTERN PIECES

Pattern piece A1, skirt front and back:
Cut two from fabric.

Pattern piece A2, optional pocket:
Cut two from fabric.

Refer to the Pattern Sheet Guide on page 152 to locate the pattern sheet number with the appropriate pieces for your garment.

CUTTING

Cut pattern pieces on the lines marked for the variation and size you are making. Transfer any markings from the pattern to the fabric.

SEWING INSTRUCTIONS

1 Mark the zipper stop point according to the pattern piece on the wrong side of the skirt front and skirt back at the skirt left side with the wash-away fabric marker or chalk. For Variation 1, or if adding pockets to Variations 2 or 3, mark the pocket placement on the skirt front.

2 Staystitch along the waist seamline, ½" (12 mm) from the cut edge.

FOR VARIATION 1 AND OPTIONAL POCKETS ONLY:

3 Press each pocket's upper edge under ½" (12 mm) and then another ¾" (2 cm). Topstitch close to the first fold.

4 Press the sides and lower edge of each pocket under ½" (12 mm).

5 With the wrong side of the pockets against the right side of the skirt front, align the pockets at the pocket placement markings and pin in place. Topstitch the pockets to the skirt front around the sides and lower edge, backstitching at each upper corner to reinforce. [A]

FOR ALL VARIATIONS:

6 Sew the skirt front and back at the side seams with right sides together, leaving the seam unsewn above the zipper marking on the left side. Press the seam allowances open. [B]

7 Staystitch the zipper opening seamline on the skirt front and skirt back.

8 Attach a zipper foot to the sewing machine and adjust the needle position so the needle is on the right side of the zipper foot. (Be sure to check the machine's instruction manual first; this position may not be recommended for your machine.)

9 Unzip the zipper. With right sides together, place the right side of the zipper on the skirt back with the top zipper stop ½" (12 mm) down from the upper raw edge of the skirt and the zipper coils just inside the staystitching line. Sew down the zipper tape, keeping the stitches close to the zipper coil but not stitching through it. Stop sewing at the zipper stop point mark and backstitch. [C]

10 Following your machine manufacturer's instructions, reattach the zipper foot while changing the needle position so that the needle is on the left side of the zipper foot. With right sides together, position the zipper's left side on the skirt front, aligning and sewing it as in Step 9. [D]

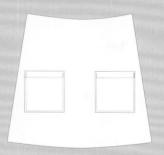

A. PIN POCKETS TO SKIRT FRONT AND STITCH IN PLACE

B. SEW TOGETHER SKIRT FRONT AND BACK, LEAVING SPACE FOR ZIPPER

C. ATTACH ZIPPER TO SKIRT BACK, STITCHING CLOSE TO COILS

D. ATTACH ZIPPER TO SKIRT FRONT

**E. ZIP CLOSED AND PRESS
SEAMS WITH COOL IRON**

**F. TOPSTICH RIBBON TO SKIRT'S
UPPER EDGE**

11 Zip the zipper and press gently, with the iron set at a cool temperature, from the right side of the skirt. (E)

12 Using the pattern piece as a guide, shape and press the ribbon to mimic the curve of the skirt waistline seam.

13 Switch back to your sewing machine's all-purpose foot. Unzip the zipper.

14 With the skirt right side up, align the ribbon along the waist staystitching with the concave edge of the ribbon on the stitching line and the convex, stretched edge pointing toward the top of the skirt. Leave ½" (12 mm) extending beyond the zipper at each end. Topstitch the ribbon very close to its concave edge, starting at the zipper opening seam allowance of the skirt back and sewing around the skirt's waist to the zipper opening seam allowance at the skirt front. (F)

15 Press the ribbon toward the inside of the skirt. Fold under the ribbon raw ends at the zipper opening, press, and whipstitch them to the zipper tape to secure.

16 Hang the skirt overnight to allow the natural bias drape to set.

FOR VARIATION 2 ONLY:

17 Topstitch the hemline 1" (2.5 cm) from the lower raw edge and trim the excess hem allowance a scant ¼" (6 mm) from the stitching line.

FOR VARIATIONS 1 AND 3:

18 Press the hem allowance up a scant ½" (12 mm), then another scant ½" (12 mm). Topstitch the hem close to the first fold.

Kiomi Top/Dress

Flowy, A-line shaped top or dress with bias-bound armhole opening and bias-bound neck edge. Top Variation 1, on page 86, uses purchased binding in a contrasting color. Mid-length dress Variation 2, on page 88, includes an optional belt and loops.

VARIATION 1:
Top

VARIATION 2:
Mid-length dress

VARIATION 3:
Maxi dress

½" (12 mm) seam allowance used unless otherwise indicated.

FABRIC CUTTING GUIDES

KIOMI TOP

MID LENGTH
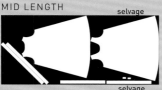

MAXI
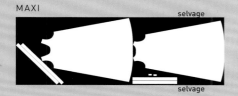

SUPPLIES

All Variations

Lightweight or mid-weight cotton, lightweight silk, handkerchief or mid-weight linen fabric

All-purpose thread

Top

1⅔ yards (1.5 m) fabric at least 44" (112 cm) wide

2 yards (1.8 m) ½"- (12 mm-) wide double-fold bias binding for top Variation 1 shown on page 86

Mid-Length Dress

2⅔ yards (2.4 m) fabric at least 44" (112 cm) wide

Maxi Dress

3⅝ yards (3.3 m) fabric at least 44" (112 cm) wide

TOOLS
· Pins
· Scissors
· Wash-away fabric marker or chalk

PATTERN PIECES
Pattern piece B1, top/dress front: Cut one from fabric on fold.

Pattern piece B2, top/dress back: Cut one from fabric on fold.

Pattern piece B3, optional top/dress neck and armhole binding: Cut two from fabric.

Pattern piece B4, optional belt: Cut two from fabric.

Pattern piece B5, optional belt loops: Cut two from fabric.

Refer to the Pattern Sheet Guide on page 152 to locate the pattern sheet number with the appropriate pieces for your garment.

CUTTING
Cut pattern pieces on the lines marked for the variation and size you are making. Transfer any markings from the pattern to the fabric.

A. GATHER THE FRONT NECKLINE

B. OPEN OUT BINDING AND
SEW TO NECKLINE

C. SEW LEFT SHOULDER SEAM
AND JOIN ENDS OF BINDING

D. FOLD BINDING OVER AND TOPSTITCH
CLOSE TO SEAM LINE

E. ATTACH BINDING TO ARMHOLE EDGES

SEWING INSTRUCTIONS

1 Gather the front neckline. Sew two rows of basting stitches between the marked dots, one ¼" (6 mm) from the raw edge and one ⅝" (1.5 cm) from the raw edge. Pull the upper thread tails to gather so the area between the dots measures as follows: For XS, 3" (7.5 cm); S, 3¼" (8.2 cm); M, 3½" (8.9 cm); L, 3¾" (9.5 cm); XL, 4" (10 cm). Place a pin at each dot and wrap the thread ends around the pins to secure temporarily. (A)

2 If making Variation 1 and using purchased bias binding, skip to step 4. Otherwise, with right sides together, sew one end of each pattern B3 bias binding together using a ¼" (6 mm) seam allowance. Press seam open.

3 Press the bias binding in half lengthwise with wrong sides together and open. Press each long edge ½" (12 mm) to the wrong side (to the center crease) and press again along the center crease to create a double-fold strip.

4 With right sides together, sew the right shoulder seam of the top/dress front to the top/dress back and press the seam allowances open.

5 Measure the neckline and cut a length of bias binding equal to the measurement.

6 Open out one long edge of the neck binding and, with right sides together, align it along the neck edge. Sew it to the neckline, with a seam allowance of ½" (12 mm). Press the seam allowances toward the binding. (B)

7 With right sides together, sew the left shoulder seam, keeping the binding extended away from the garment. Contine the shoulder seam across the free ends of the binding to join them. Press the shoulder seam allowances open. (C)

8 Fold the binding over the neckline seam allowances to the wrong side, and turn the free raw edge under along the pressed fold line. From the garment's right side, topstitch the binding close to the seamline, being sure to catch the seam allowances and the folded edge on the wrong side in the stitching. (D)

9 Measure the armhole from front side seam to back side seam and cut two lengths of bias binding to match this measurement.

10 Open one binding's center fold and enclose an armhole edge within the binding. Pin in place, then topstitch the binding close to the inner fold, being sure to catch the folded edge on the wrong side in the stitching. Repeat for the other armhole. (E)

OPTIONAL WAIST TIE:

11 Press each loop piece in half lengthwise with wrong sides facing and open. Press each long raw edge to the wrong side (to the pressed center crease) and press again along the center crease to create a double-fold strip. Topstitch close to the two folded edges to finish. **(F)**

Fold each loop in half and align the raw ends of each loop to the right and left dress front marks for loops on pattern piece B1. Stitch the loops in place ⅜" (1 cm) from the raw edge.

12 With right sides together, sew one end of each waist tie piece together using a ¼" (6 mm) seam allowance, and press seam open. Press the waist tie piece in half lengthwise and open. Press each long raw edge to the pressed center crease and press again along the center crease to create a double-fold strip. Topstitch close to the two folded edges to finish. To finish the tie ends, turn under ¼" (6 mm) and ¼" (6 mm) again and topstitch close to the first fold.

FOR ALL VARIATIONS:

13 Sew the top/dress front to the top/dress back at the side seams, with right sides together.

14 Press the hem allowance up a scant ¼" (6 mm), then another scant ½" (12 mm). Topstitch the hem close to the first pressed edge.

F. PRESS LOOP PIECE TO CREATE DOUBLE-FOLD STRIP AND STITCH

Owyn Pants/Shorts

Simple, tapered pants or shorts with flat-front waist and side/back waist elastic.

VARIATION 1:
Shorts with belt loops

VARIATION 2:
Pants

½" (12 mm) seam allowance used unless otherwise indicated.

FABRIC CUTTING GUIDES

SHORTS   PANTS

SUPPLIES

All Variations

Mid-weight cotton, woven silk/cotton/rayon blend, mid-weight linen fabric

1"- (2.5 cm-) wide elastic

All-purpose thread

Shorts with Belt loops

1 yard (90 cm) fabric at least 44" (112 cm) wide

Pants

2¼ yards (2 m) fabric at least 44" (112 cm) wide

TOOLS
· Pins
· Scissors
· Wash-away fabric marker or chalk
· Safety pin or bodkin

PATTERN PIECES

Pattern piece C1, pants/shorts front: Cut two from fabric.

Pattern piece C2, pants/shorts back: Cut two from fabric.

FOR VARIATION 1

Pattern C3, belt loops: Cut one from fabric.

Refer to the Pattern Sheet Guide on page 153 to locate the pattern sheet number with the appropriate pieces for your garment.

CUTTING

Cut the pattern pieces on the lines marked for the variation and size you are making. Transfer any markings from the pattern to the fabric.

SEWING INSTRUCTIONS

1 With right sides together, sew each shorts/pant front to the corresponding shorts/pant back at the side seam. Press the seam allowances open.

2 With right sides together, sew each pant front to the corresponding pant back at the inseam. Press the seam allowances open. [A]

3 Turn the right pant leg right side out and slip it into the left pant leg, aligning the crotch seam and matching the corresponding side and inseams. Sew the crotch seam from the front waist to the back waist. [B]

4 Remove right leg from inside left leg and turn wrong side out. Turn the waistband casing section at the upper edge of the pants/shorts to the wrong side along the line indicated on the pattern pieces and press. Open the pressed edge and press the raw edge under ¼" (6 mm).

5 Turn the waistband section to the inside of the pants/shorts and top-stitch close to the lower fold, from the front casing mark at the left side to the front casing mark on the right side.

6 Attach a safety pin or bodkin to one end of the elastic, and insert the elastic into the casing and pull it through so that ½" (12 mm) of elastic extends beyond the right front casing mark. Topstitch the elastic in place from the upper pressed edge of the casing down to the right front casing mark, backstitching to reinforce.

7 This is a good time to try on the pants. Adjust the elastic according to the comfort of the wearer, by pulling the free end at the left side of the casing.

8 Pin the elastic at the left front casing, and cut the excess, leaving ½" (12 mm) extending beyond the casing mark. Topstitch the elastic in place from the upper pressed edge of the casing down to the left front casing mark, backstitching to reinforce.

9 Topstitch the lower edge of the casing at the pants/shorts front from the left front casing mark to the right front casing mark. (C)

10 For shorts, press the hem allowance up ½" (12 mm), then another 1" (2.5 cm). Topstitch the hem close to the first pressed edge. For pants, press the hem allowance up ¼" (6 mm), then another ½" (12 mm). Topstitch the hem close to the first pressed edge.

FOR VARIATION 1 WITH BELT LOOPS:

11 Press the loop piece in half lengthwise and open. Press each long raw edge to the pressed center crease and press again along the center crease to create a double-fold strip. Topstitch close to the two folded edges to finish.

12 Cut the strip into four 2⅜" (6 cm) pieces. Press under the raw ends of each belt loop ¼" (6 mm).

13 Topstitch the loops to the shorts front and back at the marks indicated on the pattern piece. Stitch close to the fold at the top and bottom of each loop and backstitch to reinforce.

A. SEW PANT FRONTS TO PANT BACKS

B. TURN RIGHT LEG INSIDE OUT AND SLIP INTO LEFT LEG TO SEW CROTCH SEAM

C. TOPSTITCH LOWER EDGE OF CASING

Pilvi Jacket/Coat

Raglan sleeve unlined jacket or coat.

VARIATION 1:
Short length with optional folded collar detail

VARIATION 2:
Long length with inseam pockets

½" (12 mm) seam allowance used unless otherwise indicated.

FABRIC CUTTING GUIDES

JACKET   COAT

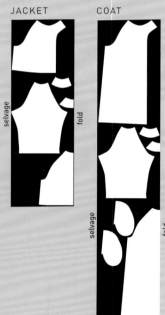

selvage   fold

selvage   fold

SUPPLIES

All Variations
Wool coating, textured mid-weight wool, mid-weight cotton fabric

All-purpose thread

Two ¾" (2 cm) buttons or snaps (optional)

Jacket
1⅞ yards (1.7 m) fabric 44" (112 cm) wide

¾ yard (68 cm) 20"- (50 cm-) wide lightweight woven fusible interfacing; Shape-Flex by Pellon recommended

Coat
3 yards (2.7 m) fabric at least 44" (112 cm) wide

1¼ yards (1.1 m) 20"- (50 cm-) wide lightweight woven fusible interfacing; Shape-Flex by Pellon recommended

TOOLS
· Pins
· Scissors
· Wash-away fabric marker or chalk

PATTERN PIECES
Pattern piece D1, jacket/coat front: Cut two from fabric.

Pattern piece D2, jacket/coat back: Cut one from fabric on fold.

Pattern piece D3, jacket/coat sleeve: Cut two from fabric.

Pattern piece D3, jacket/coat shoulder neckline facing: Cut two from fabric; cut two from interfacing following neckline facing cutting line.

Pattern piece D2, jacket/coat back neck facing: Cut one from fabric on fold; cut one from interfacing on fold following back neckline facing cutting line.

FOR VARIATION 2
Pattern piece D4, pocket: Cut four from fabric.

Refer to the Pattern Sheet Guide on page 153 to locate the pattern sheet number with the appropriate pieces for your garment. Finish all seam allowances except hems with a narrow zigzag stitch or overlock stitch before assembly.

CUTTING
Cut the pattern pieces on the lines marked for the variation and size you are making. Transfer any markings from the pattern to the fabric with the wash-away fabric marker or chalk.

SEWING INSTRUCTIONS

1 Fuse interfacing to the wrong side of the jacket front and back facing pieces, using a press cloth to protect the surface of the fabric and the iron. Follow the interfacing manufacturer's instructions for iron settings.

2 Sew the jacket back to the back of each sleeve with right sides together, and press the seams open. [A]

3 Sew each jacket front to the front of each sleeve with right sides together, and press the seams open.

4 With right sides together, sew each shoulder neckline facing to the back neck facing at each back shoulder seam, and press the seam allowances open. [B]

5 With right sides together, sew the shoulder facings to the coat front facings at the front shoulder seams, and press the seam allowances open.

6 Staystitch the neckline of the jacket and the jacket facing a scant ½" (12 mm) from the raw edge.

7 With right sides together, fold the front facing portion of the jacket front onto the jacket front and sew the joined front/shoulder/ back neck facing to the joined jacket front/sleeve/jacket back at the neck edge. Clip (see page 126) the neck edge seam allowance and trim the seam allowances to ¼" (6 mm). [C]

8 Turn the inside edge of the facing ¼" (6 mm) to the wrong side and press.

9 At the jacket's front hem, sew across the lower edge of the facing to anchor it to the jacket hemline, 1¼" (3 cm) from the lower edges. Backstitch at the edge of the facing. [D]

FOR VARIATION 1:

10 Sew the sleeve seams and jacket side seams with right sides together in one continuous seam: Start at the sleeve hem, sew to the armhole seam, pivot, and sew down the side seam. Press seams open. [E]

A. SEW THE BACK OF EACH SLEEVE TO THE JACKET BACK

B. STITCH THE SHOULDER NECKLINE FACINGS TO THE BACK NECK FACING

C. SEW THE FACING TO THE COAT AT THE NECKLINE

D. ANCHOR LOWER EDGE OF FACING TO JACKET HEMLINE

E. SEW SLEEVES AND JACKET SIDE SEAMS TOGETHER WITH ONE CONTINUOUS SEAM

F. STITCH POCKETS TO JACKET
FRONTS AND BACKS AT TOP EDGES

G. SEW SLEEVES, SIDES, AND POCKETS
WITH ONE CONTINUOUS SEAM

H. TOPSTITCH JACKET AND FACING
CLOSE TO INSIDE PRESSED EDGE

I. TOPSTITCH HEMLINE CLOSE
TO UPPER FOLD

J. STITCH BUTTON TO EACH
COLLAR POINT

FOR VARIATION 2:

11 With right sides together, match one pocket piece to each jacket front at the side seam where marked. Stitch the pockets to the fronts at their top edge. Repeat with the remaining pockets on the jacket backs. Press the pockets out away from the body of the jacket and press the seams out away from the jacket. (F)

12 Sew the sleeve seams, jacket side seams, and pocket seams with right sides together in one continuous seam: Start at the sleeve hem, sew to the armhole seam, pivot, sew down the side seam to the upper pocket dot, pivot, sew around the pocket to the lower pocket dot, pivot, and sew down the side seam to the hem. Press seams and pockets toward the coat front. (G)

FOR ALL VARIATIONS:

13 Turn the jacket facing to the inside of the jacket and press.

14 Turn the hemline ¼" (6 mm) and then a scant 1" (2.5 cm) to the wrong side and press. Pin the hem in place.

15 Pin the facing to the inside of the jacket. Topstitch the jacket and facing close to the inside pressed edge of the facing along the front opening and neck edge, in one continuous stitching line. (H)

16 Topstitch the hemline close to the upper fold, starting ¼" (6 mm) inside the pressed edge of the facing and stopping ¼" (6 mm) past the pressed edge of the opposite side front facing. (I)

17 Hem each sleeve by turning ¼" (6 mm) and then a scant 1" (2.5 cm) to the wrong side and press. Topstitch the hem close to the upper fold of the hem.

FOR VARIATION 1:

18 Fold the collar down to the outside of the jacket at the neck edge along the fold line marking on pattern piece D1, and press. Stitch the collar in place at the marking on pattern piece D1, stitching through the collar, jacket, and jacket facing to secure collar. As an optional finish, you could instead secure with a decorative button or snap. (J)

Esme Top/Tunic/Kaftan

Simple shift-shape top, tunic, and kaftan.

VARIATION 1:
Top with cap sleeve

VARIATION 2:
Top with three-quarter-length set-in sleeve

VARIATION 3:
Tunic with pockets with three-quarter-length set-in sleeve

VARIATION 4:
Tunic with three-quarter-length set-in sleeve

VARIATION 5:
Kaftan with three-quarter-length set-in sleeve
½" (12 mm) seam allowance used unless otherwise indicated.

FABRIC CUTTING GUIDES

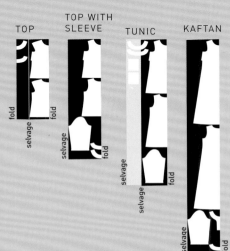

SUPPLIES

All Variations

Lightweight or mid-weight cotton, cotton double gauze, handkerchief or mid-weight linen fabric

All-purpose thread

Top with Cap Sleeve

1½ yards (1.4 m) fabric at least 44" (112 cm) wide

Top with Set-In Sleeve

2¼ yards (2 m) fabric at least 44" (112 cm) wide

Tunic

2¾ yards (2.5 m) fabric at least 44" (112 cm) wide

Kaftan

4 yards (3.6 m) fabric at least 44" (112 cm) wide:

TOOLS
· Pins
· Scissors
· Wash-away fabric marker or chalk

PATTERN PIECES

VARIATION 1, TOP WITH CAP SLEEVE

Pattern piece E1, top/tunic/kaftan front: Cut one from fabric on fold following top cutting length and cap sleeve lines.

Pattern piece E2, top/tunic/kaftan back: Cut one from fabric on fold following top cutting length and cap sleeve lines.

Pattern piece E1, top/tunic front facing: Cut one from fabric on fold following facing cutting line.

Pattern piece E2, top/tunic back facing: Cut one from fabric on fold following facing cutting line.

VARIATION 2, TOP WITH THREE-QUARTER-LENGTH SLEEVE

Pattern piece E1, top/tunic/kaftan front: Cut one from fabric on fold following top cutting length and set-in sleeve armhole lines.

Pattern piece E2, top/tunic/kaftan back: Cut one from fabric on fold following top cutting length and set-in sleeve armhole lines.

Pattern piece E3, top/tunic/kaftan sleeve: Cut two from fabric.

Pattern piece E1, top/tunic front facing: Cut one from fabric on fold following facing cutting line.

Pattern piece E2, top/tunic back facing: Cut one from fabric on fold following facing cutting line.

VARIATIONS 3 AND 4: TUNIC WITH POCKETS, TUNIC

Pattern piece E1, top/tunic/kaftan front: Cut one from fabric on fold following tunic cutting length and set-in sleeve armhole lines.

Pattern piece E2, top/tunic/kaftan back: Cut one from fabric on fold following tunic cutting length and set-in sleeve armhole lines.

Pattern piece E3, top/tunic/kaftan sleeve: Cut two from fabric.

Pattern piece E1, top/tunic front facing: Cut one from fabric on fold following facing cutting line.

Pattern piece E2, top/tunic back facing: Cut one from fabric on fold following facing cutting line.

Pattern piece A2, pockets (optional): Cut two from fabric.

VARIATION 5, KAFTAN:

Pattern piece E1, top/tunic/kaftan front: Cut one from fabric on fold following kaftan cutting length and set-in sleeve armhole lines.

Pattern piece E2, top/tunic/kaftan back: Cut one from fabric on fold following kaftan cutting length and set-in sleeve armhole lines.

Pattern piece E3, top/tunic/kaftan sleeve: Cut two from fabric.

Pattern piece E1, kaftan front facing: Cut one from fabric on fold following kaftan facing cutting line.

Pattern piece E2, top/tunic/kaftan back facing: Cut one from fabric on fold following facing cutting line.

Refer to the Pattern Sheet Guide on page 154 to locate the pattern sheet number with the appropriate pieces for your garment.

CUTTING

Transfer any markings from the pattern to the fabric.

SEWING INSTRUCTIONS

1 On the wrong side of top/tunic/kaftan front, fold the dart right sides together, matching dart legs, and pin in place. Stitch along the dart legs from the side seam toward dart point. Sew off the fold at the dart point and do not backstitch. Leave long thread tails at the dart point and tie them together to secure. Press the dart allowance toward the hem. [A]

FOR VARIATION 3 :

2 Press each pocket's upper edge ¼" (6 mm) to the wrong side and then another 1¼" (3 cm). Topstitch close to the first fold.

3 Press the sides and lower edge of each pocket ½" (12 mm) to the wrong side.

4 With the wrong side of the pockets against the right side of the tunic front, align the pockets to the pocket placement markings and pin in place. Topstitch the pockets to the tunic front around the sides and lower edge, backstitching at each upper corner to reinforce. [B]

FOR ALL VARIATIONS :

5 Sew the top/tunic/kaftan front to the top/tunic/kaftan back at the shoulder seams, with right sides together. Press the seam allowances open.

6 Sew the top/tunic/kaftan front facing to the top/tunic/kaftan back facing at the shoulder seams, with right sides together. Press the seam allowances open. Turn ¼" (6 mm) to the wrong side along the outside edge of the facing and press.

7 With right sides together, pin the facing to the neckline, matching the shoulder seams, the center fronts, and the center backs. Sew the facing to the neckline: For the kaftan version, follow the stitching line on the front facing for the front neck opening. Clip the neckline seam allowances and, for the kaftan, clip into the *V* of the neckline. Turn the facing to the inside of the top/tunic/kaftan. Press the neckline edge flat, and pin the facing to the garment along its free edge. Topstitch around the outer edge of the facing to anchor it to the garment. (C-D)

FOR VARIATION 1:

8 Press ⅛" (3 mm) and a scant ⅛" (3 mm) again to the wrong side at the sleeve hem and topstitch close to the first fold.

9 Sew the sleeve seams and top side seams in one continuous seamline, starting at the sleeve hem and sewing to the hemline.

FOR VARIATIONS 2 THROUGH 5 :

10 Sew two rows of basting stitches along the sleeve caps between the dots, one ¼" (6 mm) from the raw edge and one ¾" (2 cm) from the raw edge. (E) Ease the sleeves to fit the armhole openings and, with right sides together, pin the sleeves into the armholes. Sew the armhole seams and press the seam allowances toward the sleeve. (F)

11 Sew the sleeve seams and the top/tunic/kaftan side seams in one continuous seamline, starting at the sleeve hem, pivoting at the armhole seam, and continuing to the hemline.

12 Hem the sleeves. Press ¼" (6 mm) and 1" (2.5 cm) again to the wrong side at the sleeve hem and topstitch close to the first fold.

FOR ALL VARIATIONS:

13 Hem the top/tunic/kaftan. Press up ¼" (6 mm) and 1" (2.5 cm) again to the wrong side at the hemline and topstitch close to the first fold.

A. PIN AND SEW DARTS AND PRESS TOWARD HEM

B. ATTACH POCKETS TO TUNIC FRONT

TOP

KAFTAN
C – D. STITCH FACING TO NECKLINE

E. SEW TWO ROWS OF BASTING STITCHES ALONG SLEEVE CAPS

F. EASE THE SLEEVES AND ATTACH TO ARMHOLE OPENINGS

Elsa Everyday Tote

Unlined, rounded corner, flat tote with rivet-attached leather handles and facing. Small tote is 18" × 16" (46 × 41 cm); large tote is 24" × 24" (61 × 61 cm).

VARIATION 1:
Small

VARIATION 2:
Large

½" (12 mm) seam allowance used unless otherwise indicated.

FABRIC CUTTING GUIDES

SMALL

LARGE

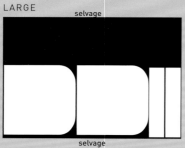

SUPPLIES
All Variations
Denim, mid-weight wool, canvas, hand-woven fabric

Two 25" (62.5 cm) leather handles

8 metal rivet sets

All-purpose thread

Small bag
⅔ yard (60 cm) fabric at least 44" (112 cm) wide

1⅓ yards (1.2 m) 20"- (50 cm-) wide mid-weight fusible woven interfacing

Large bag
1¾ yards (1.6 m) fabric at least 44" (112 cm) wide

1¾ yards (1.6 m) 44"- (112 cm-) wide mid-weight fusible woven interfacing

TOOLS
· ⅛" (3 mm) leather punch or eyelet-cutting tool
· Pins
· Rivet-setting tool
· Scissors
· Wash-away fabric marker or chalk

PATTERN PIECES
VARIATION 1, SMALL EVERYDAY BAG
Pattern piece F1, main bag: Cut two from fabric; cut two from interfacing.

Pattern piece F2, bag facing: Cut two from fabric; cut two from interfacing.

VARIATION 2, LARGE EVERYDAY BAG
Pattern piece F3, main bag: Cut two from fabric; cut two from interfacing.

Pattern piece F4, bag facing: Cut two from fabric; cut two from interfacing.

Refer to the Pattern Sheet Guide on page 155 to locate the pattern sheet number with the appropriate pieces for your garment.

CUTTING
Transfer any markings from the pattern to the fabric.

SEWING INSTRUCTIONS

1 Fuse the interfacing to the wrong side of the main bag and bag facing pieces. Follow the manufacturers instructions for iron temperature setting.

2 With right sides together, sew the facing pieces together at the side seams.

3 Turn under ¼" (6 mm) at the lower edge of the facing and press.

4 With right sides together, sew the main bag pieces together, starting at one top edge and sewing down one side, across the bottom, and back up the other side. Turn the bag right side out.

5 With right sides together, sew the bag facing to the main bag along the upper edge. (A) Turn the bag facing to the inside of the bag and press.

6 Topstitch around the bag at the upper edge and again along the lower pressed edge of the facing. (B)

7 Mark the leather handles with two dots at each end of each handle using the corresponding pattern piece F1 or F3 as a guide. Punch holes at the dot marks using a leather punch or eyelet-cutting tool.

8 Punch holes through the main bag and bag facing at the dot marks using a leather punch or eyelet-cutting tool.

9 Attach the leather handles to the main bag by applying rivets through the punched holes. Follow the rivet-setting tool's instructions for applying the rivets. (C)

A. SEW BAG FACING TO MAIN BAG ALONG UPPER EDGE

B. TOPSTITCH AROUND BAG AT UPPER EDGE AND LOWER FACING EDGE

C. ATTACH LEATHER HANDLES TO MAIN BAG WITH RIVET-SETTING TOOL

Astrid Cross-Body Bag

Lined cross-body bag with zipper opening and leather strap attached with rivets, 8½" × 9" (21.5 × 23 cm).

½" (12 mm) seam allowance used unless otherwise indicated.

FABRIC CUTTING GUIDES

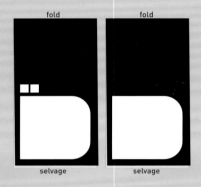

SUPPLIES

⅓ yard (30.5 cm) fabric at least 44" (112 cm) wide for outer bag: mid-weight cotton or cotton/linen recommended

⅓ yard (30.5 cm) fabric at least 44" (112 cm) wide for bag lining: mid-weight cotton or cotton/linen recommended

⅝ yard (57 cm) 20"- (50 cm-) wide woven fusible interfacing; Shape-Flex by Pellon recommended

4 sets of ¼" (6 mm) rivets

½"- to ¾"- (12 mm- to 2 cm-) wide leather strap, 47" (1.2 m) long

8" (20 cm) metal zipper with metal pull

All-purpose thread

TOOLS
· Pins
· Scissors
· ⅛" (3 mm) leather punch or eyelet-cutting tool
· Rivet-setting tool
· Fabric glue stick
· Wash-away fabric marker or chalk

PATTERN PIECES
Pattern piece G1, main bag: Cut two from fabric; cut two from interfacing; cut two from lining.

1" (2.5 cm) squares: Cut two from fabric.

Refer to the Pattern Sheet Guide on page 154 to locate the pattern sheet number with the appropriate pieces for your garment.

CUTTING
Transfer any markings from the pattern to the fabric.

SEWING INSTRUCTIONS

1 Fuse interfacing to the wrong side of the main bag pieces. Follow the manufacturer's instructions for iron temperature setting.

2 Fold each of the 1" (2.5 cm) squares in half, wrong sides together. Open the fold, and press the raw edges in to meet the first crease, and fold along the original crease, forming two 1"- (2.5-cm-) long binding pieces. Trim each end of the zipper tape above the top stop and below the bottom stop to ¼" (6 mm). Enclose the raw ends of the zipper tape at the top and bottom with the two 1" (2.5 cm) binding pieces and topstitch them in place, catching both top and bottom folds of the binding and the zipper tape all in one pass. Trim excess binding at the right and left side of the zipper. (A)

3 Sew the darts and press toward the bag bottom. Repeat with the lining fabric.

4 Fold the upper edge of each main bag piece ½" (12 mm) to the wrong side and press.

5 Apply a light layer of fabric glue to the pressed seam allowance of both main bag pieces.

6 With the wrong side of the main bag pieces facing the right side of the zipper, glue one bag piece to each side of the zipper onto the tape a scant ⅛" (3 mm) from the teeth. Center the zipper from top stop to bottom stop in the width of the main bag. Let glue dry for at least 15 minutes.

7 Attach your machine's zipper foot so that the needle is on the right side of the foot. Topstitch a main bag piece to one zipper tape, ⅛" (3 mm) from the folded edge of the main bag on the right. Repeat for the left bag side, using the left side of the zipper foot. (B)

8 Unzip the zipper halfway and, with right sides together, sew the first 4" (10 cm) of each bag side seam, starting at the upper edge. Sew each seam twice to reinforce. Press seams open.

9 Mark the leather handles with two dots at each end of each handle: one dot ⅜" (1 cm) from the end and one dot 1" (2.5 cm) from the end. Punch holes at the dot marks using a leather punch or eyelet-cutting tool.

10 Turn the bag right side out and punch holes through the main bag at the side seams at the dot marks using a leather punch or eyelet-cutting tool.

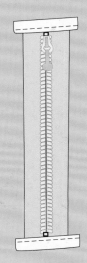

A. ATTACH BINDING PIECES TO ZIPPER

B. STITCH BAG PIECES TO ZIPPER

C. ATTACH LEATHER HANDLES TO MAIN
BAG WITH RIVET-SETTING TOOL

D. SEW LOWER PORTION OF
MAIN BAG SEAM

11 Attach the leather handles to
the main bag by applying rivets
through the punched holes.
Follow the rivet-setting tool's
instructions for applying the
rivets. (C)

12 Turn the bag inside out again
and, with right sides together,
sew the remaining lower portion
of the main bag seam, starting at
one previously stitched side seam
and sewing around the bottom of
the bag to the opposite side seam.
(D)

13 With right sides together, sew the
sides and lower seam of the bag
lining pieces.

14 Press ½" (12 mm) to the wrong
side along the upper edge of the
lining.

15 Turn the main bag wrong side
out and the lining right side out.
With wrong sides together slip
the main bag into the lining and
hand-sew the pressed upper edge
of the lining to the wrong side of
the zipper tape, a scant ¼"
(6 mm) from the zipper teeth.

16 Turn the bag right side out.

Wilma Large Tote

Unlined bag, with continuous side and bottom piece, creates a square shape if bag was stiff but the soft fabric creates more of a *V* shape, 30 × 15" (76 × 38 cm).

½" (12 mm) seam allowance used unless otherwise indicated.

FABRIC CUTTING GUIDE

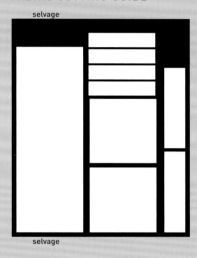

SUPPLIES

1⅜ yards (1.2 m) fabric at least 54" (137 cm) wide: heavyweight cotton or cotton/linen recommended

2⅞ yards (2.6 m) 20"- (50 cm-) wide woven fusible interfacing: Shape-Flex by Pellon recommended

All-purpose thread

TOOLS
· Pins
· Scissors
· Wash-away fabric marker or chalk

PATTERN PIECES
Pattern piece H1, center panel: Cut two from fabric; cut two from interfacing.

Pattern piece H2, sides-bottom panel: Cut one from fabric; cut one from interfacing.

Pattern piece H3, bag straps: Cut two from fabric; cut two from interfacing.

Pattern piece H4, bag facing: Cut four from fabric; cut four from interfacing.

Refer to the Pattern Sheet Guide on page 155 to locate the pattern sheet number with the appropriate pieces for your garment.

CUTTING
Transfer any markings from the pattern to the fabric and interfacing.

A. STITCH SEAMS ON CENTER
PANEL PIECES

B. SEW CENTER PANELS TO SIDES A
AND B OF SIDE/BOTTOM PANEL

C. REPEAT FOR OPPOSITE CENTER
PANEL AND AND SIDE/BOTTOM PANEL

D. MATCH BAG AND FACING
SEAMS AND SEW

SEWING INSTRUCTIONS

1 Fuse interfacing to the wrong side of the bag pieces. Follow the manufacturer's instructions for the iron temperature setting.

2 Staystitch along the stitch lines on either side of the four dots marked on the bag sides/bottom panel.

3 Clip into the seam allowance almost to the staystitching at each of the dots marked on the bag sides/ bottom panel.

4 With right sides together and raw edges aligned, match the dots on the lower edge of one of the center panel pieces to the dots on one long side of the bag sides/bottom panel. Sew the seam between the dots. (A) Repeat with the other center panel piece and the opposite long side of the bag sides/bottom panel.

5 Sew one side of one center panel to the side A seam section of the bag side/bottom panel; sew from upper edge of center panel and stop at dot. Sew the opposite side of the same center panel to the side B seam section of the bag side/bottom panel in the same fashion. (B) Repeat for the opposite center panel and bag side/bottom panel. Finish the seam allowances with narrow zigzag stitch. (C)

6 With right sides together, sew the four facing pieces short end to short end, creating one continuous length. Join the short ends to create a loop.

7 Double-fold and press the strap pieces along the fold lines, enclosing the raw edges. Topstitch along both long edges of each strap ⅛" (3 mm) from the edges.

8 Turn the bag right side out. With right sides together and raw edges aligned, pin the ends of one strap to the bag on one center panel, aligning the outside edges of the strap ends with the center panel/bag side/bottom panel seams. Repeat with the remaining strap and center panel. The straps should hang down toward the bottom of the bag.

9 Turn the lower edge of the bag facing ½" (12 mm) to the wrong side and press.

10 With right sides together and raw edges aligned, pin the facing to the upper edge of the bag; match the seams of the bag and facing. Sew this seam, catching the strap ends. Press the facing to the inside of the bag and topstitch the bag/facing at the upper edge and ⅛" (3 mm) from the pressed lower edge of the facing. (D) *Optional: Topstitch parallel rows of stitching within the width of the facing every ¼" (6 mm) to create an extra sturdy and decorative finish.

11 Turn the bag right side out.

Cecilia Yoga Bag

Unlined canvas yoga bag with shaped, faced strap and upper edges, 12" × 35½" (30.5 cm × 90 cm).

½" (12 mm) seam allowance used unless otherwise indicated.

FABRIC CUTTING GUIDE

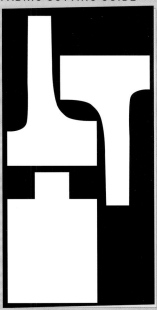

selvage

SUPPLIES

1¼ yards (1.1 m) fabric at least 44" (112 cm) wide: cotton or cotton/linen canvas recommended

All-purpose thread

TOOLS
· Pins
· Scissors
· Wash-away fabric marker or chalk

PATTERN PIECES
Pattern piece I1, lower bag: Cut two from fabric.

Pattern piece I2, strap section: Cut four from fabric.

Refer to the Pattern Sheet Guide on page 156 to locate the pattern sheet number with the appropriate pieces for your garment.

CUTTING
Transfer any markings from the pattern to the fabric.

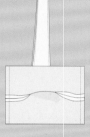

A. SEW STRAP PAIRS TOGETHER ALONG LONG UPPER EDGE

B. OPEN STRAP LAYERS AND STITCH SIDE SEAMS TOGETHER

C. SEW BAG BOTTOM SEAM

SEWING INSTRUCTIONS

1 Sew one pair of strap pieces together at the top of the strap and press the seam open. Repeat with the remaining strap pair.

2 With right sides together sew one strap pair to the other strap pair along the long upper edge and curved strap sides. (A) Clip the curved seam allowances and turn right side out through the strap.

3 Open the outer strap and inside strap layers at each strap lower section and with right sides together sew the side seams of the two strap sections together. Press the seam allowances open. (B)

4 Topstitch the finished edges of the straps/bag opening.

5 With right sides together, sew the side seams of the main bag and finish the seam allowances with a narrow zigzag stitch.

6 With right sides together sew the bag bottom seam. Finish the seam allowance with a narrow zigzag stitch. (C)

7 With right sides together, sew the two bottom gussets. Align the bag bottom seam line with the side seams. Stitch this seam twice to reinforce. Finish seams with a narrow zigzag stitch. Keep the lower bag turned wrong side out. (D)

8 Sew the outer strap section to the lower bag. Slip the strap section down into the lower bag, strap first, aligning the upper edge of the lower bag to the lower edge of the bag's outside strap section. With the right side of the lower bag facing the right side of the outer bag strap section, align the raw edges and side seams. Sew this seam, catching only the lower bag and the outer strap section. Pull the strap up out of the bag and press the seam toward the upper bag.

9 Press up ½" (12 mm) to the wrong side of the lower edge of the inside strap section and pin the folded edge to the seam sewn in step 8 so that it covers the seam allowances. Topstitch the seam ⅛" (3 mm) above the finished seamline to secure the inside strap section and finish the bag. (E)

D. CREATE BOTTOM GUSSETS

E. FINISH SEAM LINE TO SECURE
INSIDE STRAP SECTION

Pattern Sheet Guides

All of the pattern pieces for the garments in this book are included on two numbered, double-sided pattern sheets attached to the back of the book. The guides here show at a glance where the pieces for each garment are located within these pattern sheets.

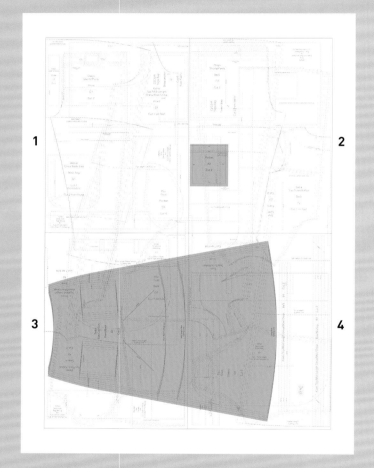

TEDRA SKIRT

Pattern sheets 2, 3, and 4

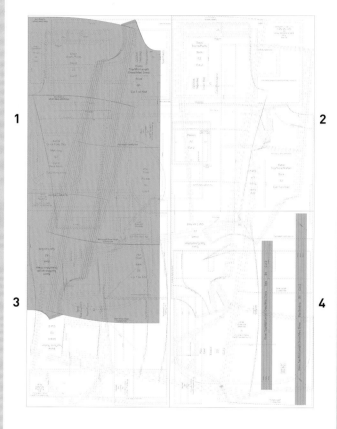

KIOMI TOP/DRESS

Pattern sheets 1, 3, and 4

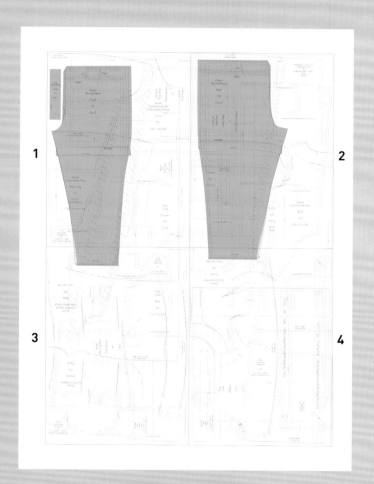

OWYN PANTS/SHORTS

Pattern sheets 1, 2, 3, and 4

PILVI JACKET/COAT

Pattern sheets 1, 2, 3, and 4

Pattern Sheet Guides

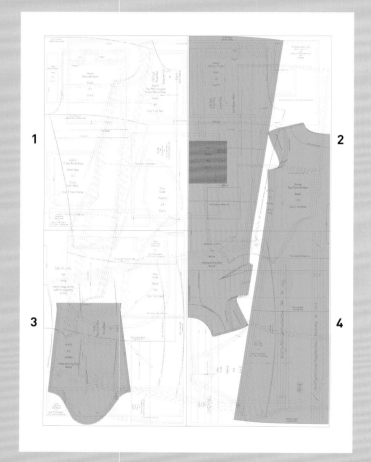

ESME TOP/TUNIC/KAFTAN

Pattern sheets 2, 3, and 4

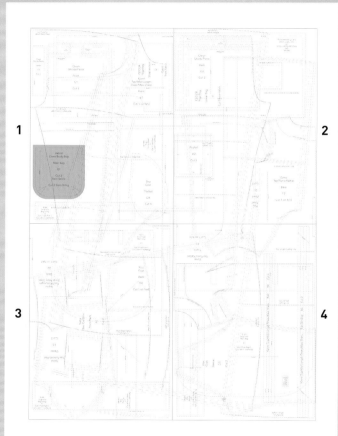

ASTRID CROSS-BODY BAG

Pattern sheet 1

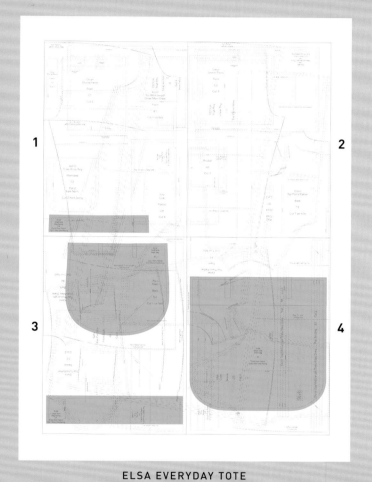

ELSA EVERYDAY TOTE

Pattern sheets 1, 3, and 4

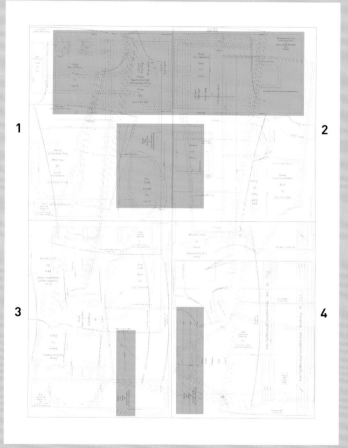

WILMA LARGE TOTE

Pattern sheets 1, 2, 3, and 4

Pattern Sheet Guides

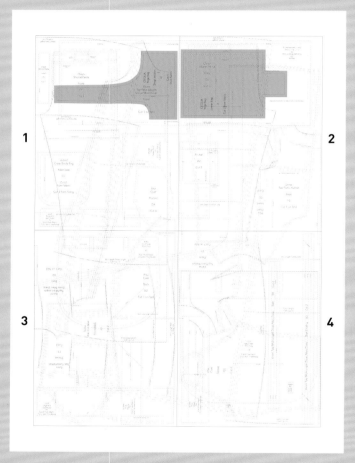

CECILIA YOGA BAG

Pattern sheets 1 and 2

Resources

Contributors

I design and make many different products, write books, and also teach workshops. If you want to learn more about what I'm doing, please visit my website.
jansdotter.com

I love to design fabric collections and I do that with great pleasure and joy with Windham Fabrics. They are a family company based in New Jersey and they are the nicest and most fun people to work with. Please visit their website to learn more about our past, current, and future fabric collections.
windhamfabrics.net

Jenny Hallengren, this book's photographer, is remarkably talented and one of the hardest working people I know. Do visit her site to see more of her work.
jennyhallengren.se

Alexia Abegg is a talented seamstress and fabric designer and is creative in many other ways; she is a Renaissance woman. Check out her site to see what she is working on now.
alexiaabegg.squarespace.com

Fabric

I source fabric from many different places. In New York City, we have some amazing stores that have been around for decades. These are three of my favorites.

B&J FABRICS
525 Seventh Avenue
New York, NY 10018
(212) 354-8150
bandjfabrics.com

MOOD DESIGNER FABRICS
225 W. 37th Street
New York, NY 10018
(212) 730-5003
moodfabrics.com

ROSEN & CHADICK FABRICS
561 Seventh Avenue
New York, NY 10018
(212) 869-0142
rosenandchadickfabrics.com

Find Out More

PAGES 4–5
Ah, yes, all those wonderful scissors. As you have probably already guessed, they are flea market and yard sale finds. Most of them are from Sweden and some are hand-me-downs.

PAGES 6–8
My vintage Featherweight Singer sewing machine is my go-to machine for all projects, even though it only does straight stitch. Actually, I have to admit I have two (one black and one white). I love that these machines are all metal, small and portable, and rather cute. Search for these old machines online.
The checkered fabric is a design of mine called Olavi.

PAGE 19
Many of my fabrics are shown here in these piles. Some I created several years ago in Japan, and some I created more recently with Windham Fabrics.

PAGE 20
This fabric is called Etapp; it is one of my designs from the Lucky collection that I designed after my trip to India.

PAGES 22–23
You can find more information about buying handwoven fabric from Camphill Soltane at camphillsoltane.org.

PAGE 26
I use very simple Moleskine notebooks as well as some handbound custom-made sketchbooks.

PAGE 31
For jewelry parts and hardware, I recommend your local bead store (if you are lucky enough to have one in your town), Etsy (etsy.com), or Fire Mountain Gems (firemountaingems.com).

PAGE 35
Annika is wearing one of her classic "A" letter necklaces from her own collection. Visit byboe.com to get your favorite letter.

PAGE 39
This Esme top was sewn out of my Olavi fabric.

PAGES 38–41
I found my mixed beads, bells, and string in funky thrift stores and at yard sales. I made some of the porcelain pieces by hand.

PAGE 44
This is my fabric design called Pav, which has been printed in many different colors throughout the years.

PAGE 46
Maria makes the best illustrations in her unique style. See her work at raymondsdotter.com.

PAGES 48–51
All the wonderful yarn we used for these pompom projects came from Purl Soho. Visit their website at purlsoho.com/purl.

PAGE 52
I bought the rather fancy and cozy wool I used for these mitts at B & J fabrics in New York (see page 157).

PAGE 55
If you want to own your own pair of traditional Scandinavian *Lovikka* mittens, they are fairly easy to find and purchase by searching online. Or try knitting your own!

PAGE 56

I bought the orange linen for these pants at Fog Linen Work. Visit their shop at foglinenwork.com.

PAGE 62

This is my Caris fabric design.

PAGE 64

This wonderful striped linen came from Fog Linen Work. Visit their shop at foglinenwork.com.

PAGES 66–67

These are my favorite, favorite boots. They were made by an Italian company called Fiorentini + Baker (fiorentini-baker.com).

Alexia got her chambray from Robert Kaufman (robertkaufman.com).

PAGES 68–69

This coat is made from my Redig fabric.

PAGES 72–73

I got my fabrics for my scarf from Fog Linen Work (foglinenwork.com), and also used a kitchen cloth that I got at the Japanese home goods store Muji (muji.com) several years ago.

PAGES 74–75

To learn more about what the very talented, wicked smart, and fun ladies who sewed these scarves do and make, you can visit their sites here:
fancytigercrafts.com
christinehaynes.com
carolynfriedlander.com

PAGES 78–79

Patty's Esme tunic is sewn out of my Lina fabric.

Every time I visit my in-laws in Mystic, Connecticut, I want go out to eat codfish and chips at Sea Swirl, a charming, simple shack by the river (seaswirlofmystic.com).

PAGES 80–81

All the pompom trim in this book came from Purl Soho (purlsoho.com).

I bought all these fabrics in India except for the chambray, which came from Robert Kaufman (robert-kaufman.com).

PAGES 82–83

These are my favorite sneakers. They are made by an Italian company called Superga (superga-usa.com).

You can find bias tape makers for various widths in most good sewing shops.

PAGES 86–87

Please visit Paula's website to learn more about her work at paulagreif-ceramics.com.

PAGES 88–89

I got this classic black washed silk in a fabric store in Nashville, but I bet you can get yours pretty much anywhere.

Learn more about Nerissa's musical gigs and other creative adventures at crookedmouthmusic.com.

PAGES 90–91

This pure Lithuanian linen fabric came from Fog Linen Work (foglinenwork.com).

PAGES 92–93

I found the handwoven rag rug we used to make this bag online. There are lots of choices on Etsy (etsy.com).

PAGE 96

This is my Hemendu fabric.

PAGES 92–93

The Kiomi Dress is made in my Finn fabric.

PAGES 100–101

I have many different watercolor sets. This is a high-quality Van Gogh travel set.

PAGES 104–105

The Pilvi jacket was sewn using my Korkekk fabric.

If you are really curious about princess cake, they actually have them in the frozen food section at Ikea in individual sizes. I must admit, they are surprisingly tasty. They also serve them in their café.

PAGES 108–109

I got this Japanese gauze Nani Iro fabric at Purl Soho (purlsoho.com).

Go and see what Anna Linda is up to at www.inflow.se.

PAGES 110–111

I got the fabulous thick, heavy linen fabric used for this bag from Fog Linen Work (foglinenwork .com).

PAGES 114–115

The porcelain mug is indeed a Lotta Jansdotter mug, but it is out of print, I am afraid.

I found the trim shown here at a flea market in the sticks in Sweden.

PAGES 116–117

Do visit Yūnmee's website to learn more about her beautiful and interesting work at yunmee.com.

Acknowledgments

Making a book is a true journey. It is so exciting to see ideas that have been bopping around in my head come alive on pages in a book that will find its ways into shops and libraries all over the world. It is especially rewarding when readers feel inspired and encouraged.

Making *Lotta Jansdotter Everyday Style* was fun, challenging, and, yes, a remarkable amount of work. It has been a year and a half of ideas, conversations, decisions, changes, writing, editing, photography, and design. I have treasured this time as it has given me the opportunity to work with a team of rather amazing individuals who clearly love and are dedicated to what they do.

I am so happy to work once again with photographer Jenny Hallengren. She and I have a wonderful professional relationship based on our deep friendship. We have known each other since we were 10 years old, which is also when we did our first photo shoot together. We are such a good team: She is where I am not, and vice versa. I am swift, hot-headed, and make quick art direction decisions. She is steady, thorough, and patient, and makes sure we always have that extra shot, just in case. And, of course, she has that amazing eye and the talent to take wonderful photos that are warm, lovely, and tell the story I want to tell. I think we can all agree that this book is just as much about Jenny's work as mine. Thank you, Jenny. This is something I simply could not have done—or would not have wanted to do—without you.

This is the first book I have created with the much talented and knowledgeable Melanie Falick. Melanie is so passionate and dedicated to her work as an editor and she has such a strong and clear vision. It is very inspiring and rewarding to work with you, Melanie, and I admire you immensely. Thank you for all your support. I hope this book is one of many more that I get to create with you.

Deb Wood is my favorite graphic design wizard in the world. She always seems to understand what I envision and want to do, even at times when I don't know it myself. She is remarkable. Thank you, Deb, for your incredible contribution to this book, your tireless work, and for you special wizardry. I hope we can do it again!

Special thanks to Nerissa Campbell, who is my "best-est" and "most-est" in so many ways. You always, I mean always, have my back, and I am so deeply grateful and lucky to have you in my life.

Alexia Abegg, thank you ever so much for making this happen, in the most professional, sweet, and lovely way. You are a remarkable lady.

A real big thank you to all the lovely models in this book. You made it come alive and awesome in the best way.

Thanks also to Cristina Garces, Nick Anderson, David McCormick, Johanna Lenander, Cree LeFavour, Michelle Abegg, Tim Utkutug, Angela Ritchie, Andrea Hernandez and the whole team at Leggoreta + Hernandez, Yumiko Sekine, Patty Anderson for your sewing help, Maja Schelski, Anita Hallengren, Joelle Hoverson and Page Norman and the wonderful staff at Purl Soho, Heather Ross for introducing me to Melanie, Makenna Howard, and my team at Windham.

Finally, I also want to take this opportunity to sincerely thank all of you: the makers, seamstresses, and fabric store owners in the world who have supported me and my work for so many years now. What is all of this without you? I am so happy to be a part of this wonderful community.

Tusen TACK ! Thank you!

Published in 2015 by Stewart, Tabori & Chang
An imprint of ABRAMS

Text and illustrations copyright © 2015 Lotta Jansdotter
Photographs copyright © 2015 Jenny Hallengren

Library of Congress Control Number: 2014959123

ISBN: 978-1-61769-174-4

Editor: Melanie Falick
Designer: Deb Wood
Production Manager: True Sims

The text of this book was composed in DIN and
Times New Roman.

Printed and bound in China

10 9 8 7 6 5 4 3 2 1

Stewart, Tabori & Chang books are available at special
discounts when purchased in quantity for premiums and
promotions as well as fundraising or educational use. Special
editions can also be created to specification. For details, con-
tact specialsales@abramsbooks.com or the address below.

THE ART OF BOOKS SINCE 1949
115 West 18th Street
New York, NY 10011
www.abramsbooks.com